SKATEBOARD

Retrospective

A Collector's Guide

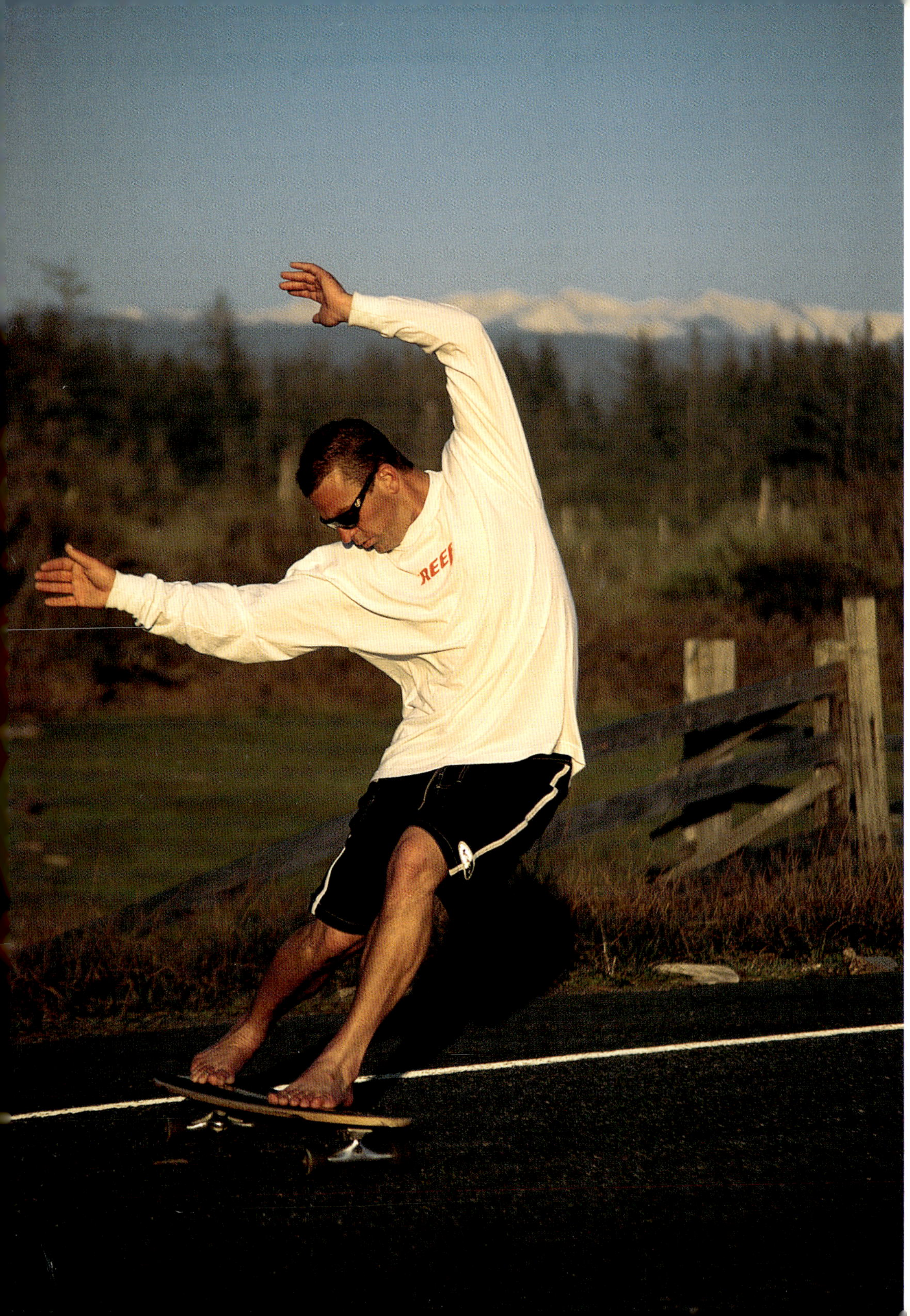

4880 Lower Valley Road, Atglen, PA 19310 USA

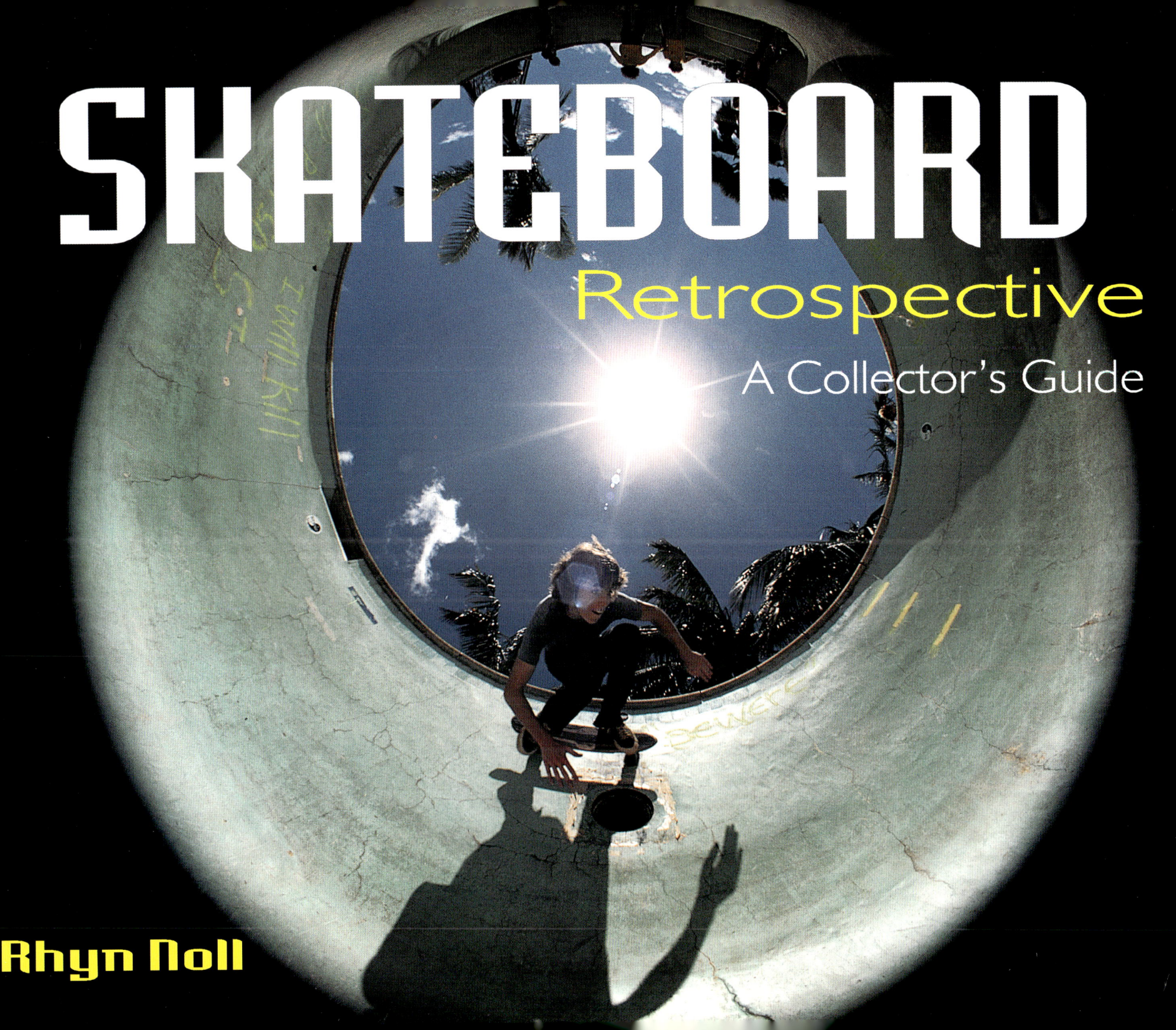

SKATEBOARD

Retrospective

A Collector's Guide

Rhyn Noll

Disclaimer

The text and products featured in this book are from the collection of the author of this book and various private collectors. This book is not sponsored, endorsed, or otherwise affiliated with any of the companies whose products are represented herein. This book is derived from the author's independent research.

Published by Schiffer Publishing Ltd.
4880 Lower Valley Road
Atglen, PA 19310
Phone: (610) 593-1777; Fax: (610) 593-2002
E-mail: Schifferbk@aol.com
Please visit our web site catalog at www.schifferbooks.com or write for a free catalog.

We are always looking for authors to write books on new and related subjects. If you have an idea for a book, please contact us at the above address.
This book may be purchased from the publisher. Please include $3.95 for shipping.

In Europe, Schiffer books are distributed by
Bushwood Books
6 Marksbury Ave.
Kew Gardens
Surrey TW9 4JF England
Phone: 44 (0)208 392-8585; Fax: 44 (0)208 392-9876
E-mail: Bushwd@aol.com
Free postage in the UK. Europe: Air mail at cost.
Please try your bookstore first.

Designed by Bonnie M. Hensley
Type set in Bedrock/Hunamist 521 BT

ISBN: 0-7643-1122-0
Printed in China
1 2 3 4

Dedication

I dedicate this book to my family. Without them I could not have accomplished it. Sarah Campbell, my sweetheart; Remy Noll, my daughter; Dane Noll, my son; Beverly Noll, my mother; Ira Roberts, my Grandpa; Bettie Roberts, my Granny; Tate Noll, my brother; Jed Noll, my brother; Ashlyne Whaley, my sister; Laura Noll; Greg Noll, my dad; Jim Noll, my uncle; Nancy Noll, my aunt; A.J. Noll, my nephew; Luke Noll, my nephew; Steve Zalaback, my uncle; Grace Noll, my Grandma; Ash Noll, my Grandpa; and Kyler Whaley

Preface

During the late 1960s my dad brought home a laminated-deck clay-wheel skateboard for me and my brother Tate. Not long after he gave it to us, he took it away, claiming it was too dangerous. Well, somehow we got hold of some wheels and trucks and we started building our own boards. We rode them down Riviera Way in Torrance, California, where I was born in 1962. Later my pals and I rode all the local streets. One place, I particularly remember was called the Riviera Bowl. It was behind the local school and was my first concrete wave experience. It was only a couple feet high on one end, tapering up gradually to several feet high at the other end. It had a great curve at the top and super transitions. We didn't charge at the incline; instead, we would hug the face, basically riding the bowl like a wave. We dropped in from the top and acted like we were surfing in a wave. Reese Patterson is one of the guys that comes to mind when I think about the old days at the bowl. Some of my other pals at this time were Darrold Hartland, Kevin McKinsie, Casey, and Mitch.

I live in Northern California now, where in 1994, I started the Noll Streetsurfer Company to manufacture skateboards. I have witnessed the entire history of the skateboard and the evolution of modern boards, wheels, and trucks. I have skated in and out of all these eras.

I guess it is in the blood. I was brought up in the industry, with my father, Greg Noll, being a pioneer surfer, surfboard builder and retailer, and among the first ever to sell skateboards. I also own a Surf Shop and have been retailing skateboards for twelve years. I have been at the forefront of the newest skateboard development, the longboard revolution.

It was my father who taught me to appreciate the history of this great sport and the collectibility of the boards and other memorabilia surrounding them. He has instilled in me the ideals that have lead to the project of creating this book.

Acknowledgments

The last 100 years of skateboarding history would not be possible if it were not for a group of collectors, historians, skaters and skate companies. A lot of great guys and gals, my publisher (for having faith) and a whole team of people contributed to this project, some of whom I would like to mention:

Todd Huber of Skatelab, one of the largest skate museums (2000 boards!) and skate parks, located in Simi Valley. Tom Craig, collector, pro skater, and keeper of history. Rich Novak of NHS, Santa Cruz, historian and skateboard company founder. Jim Phillips of Phillips Art Studios. Ed Economy, collector, historian, pro skater, and visionary. Dale Smith, pro skater and historian. Leroy Grannis, photographer and historian. Skip Engblom, skater and board manufacturer. Jack Oneill, owner of Oneill Company and historian. Warren Bolster, photographer, historian. Tim Piumarta of NHS, historian and innovator of skate design. Hobie Alter, one of the first manufacturers, visionaries, and skateboard icons. Jeff Alter, now running Hobie Co. James O'Mahoney, historian, collector, photographer, publisher. Bill at "Bill's Wheels," skate shop owner and historian. NHS Pro Skateboarders. Gary Holley, shaper, historian, manufacturer. Liz Barbee, computer operator, typist, editor, literary magician, without whom I would not have gotten this to the publisher. Linda Pearcey, researcher, internet master. Beverly Noll (my mom!), historian, surf shop owner. Bettie Roberts, my Granny, literary magician. Sarah Campbell, my sweetheart, encourager, sympathizer, and inspiration. Steve Wilkings, photographer and visionary. Randy Beck, surf shop owner, historian. Bob Pearson, surf shop owner, shaper, and manufacturer. Shyilo Stinethal, skater, manufacturer. Matt McNertney, manufacturer. Rodney Dean, book contributor. Mike Gosenski, collector. Randi Economy. Gravity Skate Board Company. Skaters from all eras and styles. Paul Gallegos. Jim Noll. Toni Pelton. Bill Weakley. Gene Cooper. Ron Gastenu of Visual Impressions. Rhyn Noll's Streetsurfer™ Company. ET Surfboards. Uncle Eddie. Greg Forsht. Osiris Skateboard Company. *International Longboard Magazine*. Kirt McKlave. Greg Noll. Laura Noll. Randal Trucks. Remy Noll. Dane Noll. Jack Smith. Hotline Wesuit Co. Reef Co. Jed Noll. Doug Harnden. Black Fly Eyewear Co. Cleve Gardner.

Contents

Introduction

The skateboard is an incredible thing: wheels, in their simplest form, connected to a piece of wood, creating a potential for transportation that is almost limitless. The needed energy is stored within the rider and once released, by a push of the foot—gravity's force creates motion and speed. The skill and courage of the individual rider create the excitement and beauty of the sport.

In my search to find the holy grail of skateboards, one thing has become clear—kids were there from the beginning. Early in the twentieth century, they were the first to attach roller skate wheels to a board to make a tee-bar scooter. Even before that, it is likely that kids were using roller skates this way from the time they were invented by Joseph Warland. His in-line skate was patented in Belgium in 1759. In 1853 independent trucks and rollerskates as we know them were manufactured.

With the first ball bearing skating wheels, kids were really rolling. They took their roller skates apart and adapted them to boards with an orange crate on top and a horizontal stick to steer with. They could push them along like scooters. It is no mystery that scooters and other strange anomalies from early manufacturers are the skateboard's predecessors.

Some consider history to be a dead issue. I believe just the opposite—if you do not remember your roots you have no culture, no real recollection or pride in what you do and why you do it.

The more I penetrate the roots of skateboards, it becomes clear that they are more than just toys for kids to play on. They are representative of America's youth, created out of their need for a mode of transportation. It was that simple, simple as the times in which they were created. Yet skateboarding is an individualistic activity—allowing kids to be mobile in their own creative way. Because of this creativity, skateboarding grows from those simple roots into the increasingly complex sport with boards that reflect that complexity. It is like a family tree that branches out in many directions, moving from the kid's orange crate street scooter, to all the skateboard's siblings, to the surfers, to big business.

Telling the story of skateboarding is like telling the story of American History.

Chapter 1

1900–1949

•1903: Orville Wright made his historical flight, and mankind took to the air.

•1914: World War I began

•1915: Einstein perfected his Theory of Relativity.

Who Did it First?

As I traced wheels on boards back as far as I could, the names that came up were Doc Ball, Harold Meserve, and Neal McMulliam. Through Doc Ball we can make a living connection with the past century. Doc Ball was 9 or 10 years old in 1918, when Harold, Neal, and he put broken roller skates on pieces of wood. They put a handle bar across the front and rode around on one knee, pushing off with the opposite foot. Doc says it was for fun and transportation, and he rode scooters and skaters of all sorts during the next few decades. It is possible that Doc is the oldest living skater to date, and he still skates today! Sadly we did not have access to his old skate photos but did get hold of some of his recent shots.

Doc Ball with his skateboard. *Photo: Rhyn Noll*

Doc Ball demonstrating how to skate on one knee and push off with the other foot in the old days. *Courtesy Doc Ball.*

Doc Ball, "Slow Children at Play." *Courtesy Doc Ball.*

Doc Ball speeding in front of his home. *Photo courtesy of Leroy Grannis.*

Doc Ball going for a downtown cruise in Eureka California, 1999. *Courtesy Doc Ball.*

Doc in an early wet suit. *Courtesy Doc Ball.*

Doc Ball accepting honors at his video screening, 1999. *Photo: Rhyn Noll*

Doc in his flight suit, World War II. *Courtesy Doc Ball.*

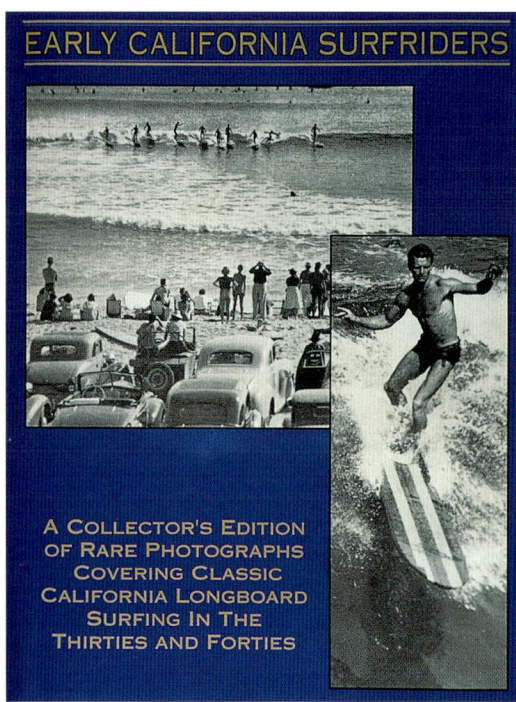

Early California Surf Riders, one of Doc Ball's publications. *Courtesy Doc Ball.*

• 1933: Prohibition ended.

In 1936 a man named Scharone patented a skateboard. In 1939 a three-wheeled scooter skate with machine-pressed steel wheels was produced, a product linked to the name of Petermann. Patents were submitted on wheels as early as 1884, as they were in 1937 by a man named Schmidt. Germany was also making roller skate wheels and in 1933 an independent truck was made for use on roller skates.

What some might consider to be the Holy Grail of Skateboards, manufactured sometime in the late 1930s. Out of the pedal car era, this toy is something you might see in an *Our Gang* comedy. At this time, surfing and board sports as we know them were still in their infancy. Kneeling around on the latest toy was most likely for the upper class and evidently the hip trip. *Courtesy Randy Beck. Photo: Rhyn Noll.*

Everett, Washington, 1928. *Courtesy Dale Smith.*

Deck logo of Busy Kiddie. *Courtesy Randy Beck. Photo: Rhyn Noll*

Young man in his classic whites on his three-wheeled scooter. *Courtesy Todd Huber.*

Randy Beck in his shop in Chadsworth, with the oldest known skateboard. Randy acquired this skateboard from an antiques dealer in Pennsylvania with Art Decofinders. This board was conceived during the depression. *Courtesy Randy Beck. Photo: Rhyn Noll*

United States Patent [19]
Johnson

[11] 4,176,850
[45] Dec. 4, 1979

[54] SKATEBOARD TRUCK WITH INDEPENDENT WHEEL SUSPENSION

[76] Inventor: Robert D. Johnson, 7882 Cedar Lake Ave., San Diego, Calif. 92119

[21] Appl. No.: 917,871

[22] Filed: Jun. 22, 1978

Related U.S. Application Data

[63] Continuation-in-part of Ser. No. 844,973, Oct. 25, 1977.

[51] Int. Cl.² A63C 17/02
[52] U.S. Cl. .... 280/87.04 A; 280/11.28
[58] Field of Search .... 280/11.28, 11.27, 87.04 A, 280/87.04 R, 11.19, 11.1 BT; 47.11, 98, 99, 100, 11.23

[56] **References Cited**
U.S. PATENT DOCUMENTS

304,949	9/1884	Mitchell	280/11.19
2,039,153	4/1936	Edwards	280/11.28
2,079,185	5/1937	Schmidt	280/11.28
4,062,557	12/1977	Roden	280/11.27 X

FOREIGN PATENT DOCUMENTS

492509 3/1954 Italy 280/11.23

Primary Examiner—Joseph F. Peters, Jr.
Assistant Examiner—Milton L. Smith
Attorney, Agent, or Firm—Flehr, Hohbach, Test, Albritton & Herbert

[57] **ABSTRACT**

A skateboard is provided with trucks, each of which carries a plurality of wheels mounted in independent suspension. Longitudinally extending swing arms carry the wheel axles forwardly or rearwardly through a yoke mounted under the skateboard by a pivot connection and by a resilient support. The arms are resiliently biased by means of separate springs or torsion bars so that varying pressures across the skateboard platform alter the distance of the skateboard wheels from the underside of the platform and conversely roadway irregularities displace the skateboard wheels towards the platform independently one from another. In one embodiment the swing arms are mounted such that the wheel axles extend substantially across the axis of the resilient support.

10 Claims, 19 Drawing Figures

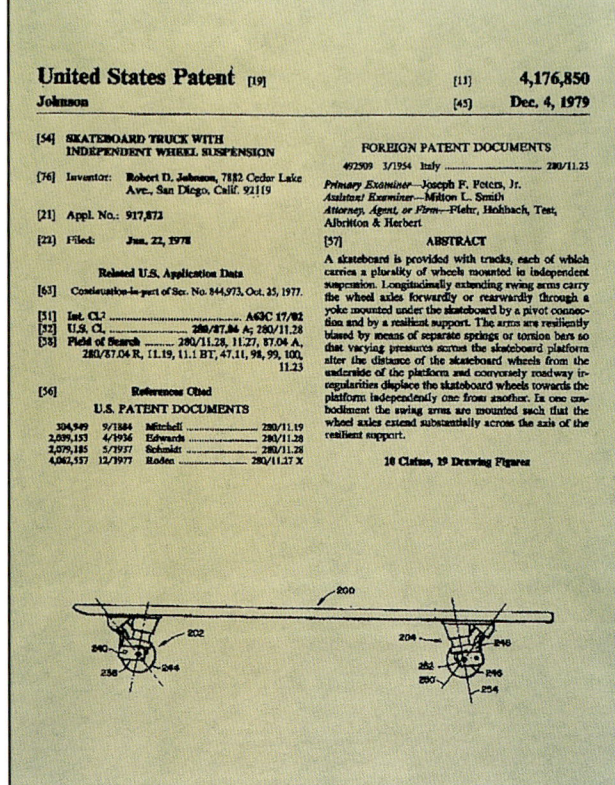

United States Patent [19]
Smisek

US005267743A

[11] Patent Number: 5,267,743
[45] Date of Patent: Dec. 7, 1993

[54] LOW PROFILE SKATEBOARD

[76] Inventor: Brandon T. Smisek, 223 Flower St., Costa Mesa, Calif. 92627

[21] Appl. No.: 794,406

[22] Filed: Nov. 19, 1991

[51] Int. Cl.⁵ A63C 17/01
[52] U.S. Cl. 280/87.042; 280/79.11; 280/87.041
[58] Field of Search 280/87.042, 87.041, 280/87.03, 87.02, 87.01, 79.11, 32.6

[56] **References Cited**
U.S. PATENT DOCUMENTS

251,000	12/1883	Peeler	280/11.2
3,843,146	10/1974	Hiraki	280/11.2
4,061,350	12/1977	Schmidt, Jr. et al.	280/87.04 A
4,151,891	5/1979	Francken	180/77
4,168,842	9/1979	Kimmel et al.	280/11.28
4,180,278	12/1979	Gottlieb	280/87.04 A
4,234,204	11/1980	Tibbals	280/87.04 A
5,022,670	6/1991	Cota et al.	280/32.6

5,067,058 11/1991 Standley 280/87.042

FOREIGN PATENT DOCUMENTS

892715 10/1953 Fed. Rep. of Germany .. 280/79.11
2416027 10/1979 France 280/87.042
8701297 3/1987 World Int. Prop. O. 280/87.042

Primary Examiner—Eric D. Culbreth
Attorney, Agent, or Firm—Graham & James

[57] **ABSTRACT**

A skateboard employs a hollow elongated board having openings, formed in the underside of the board, adapted to receive standard skateboard wheels. Since the wheels are recessed in the board, the skateboard sits very low to the ground, giving the board a low profile and low center of gravity. The skateboard further employs wheel ramps on opposite sides of each wheel to provide a smooth under surface to aid in the negotiation of large obstacles such as curbs, stairs, etc. and to allow the skateboard to glide over smaller obstacles.

17 Claims, 5 Drawing Sheets

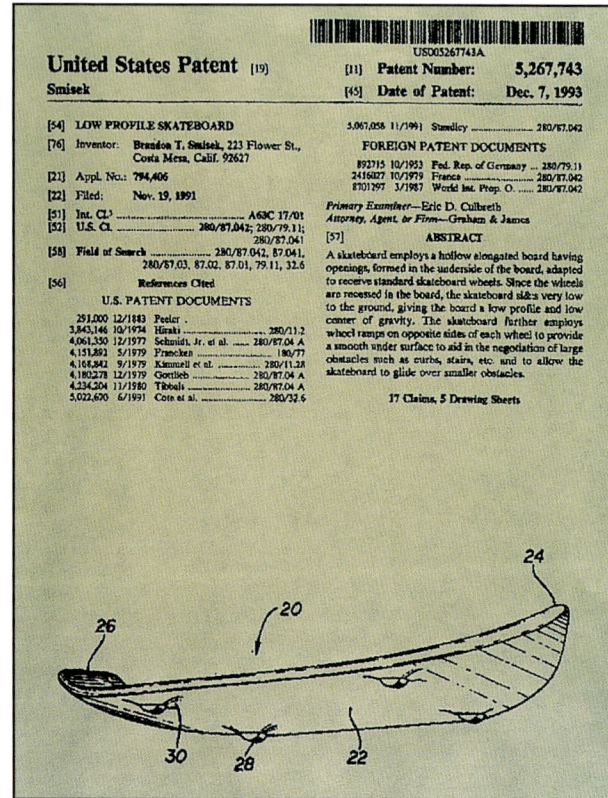

United States Patent [19]
Blackburn et al.

[11] 4,149,735
[45] Apr. 17, 1979

[54] SKATEBOARD PIVOT ROLLER

[76] Inventors: Ian Blackburn, 16081 Gold Cir., Huntington Beach, Calif. 92647; Robert V. Blackburn, 11542 Luzon St., Cypress, Calif. 90630

[21] Appl. No.: 837,893

[22] Filed: Sep. 29, 1977

[51] Int. Cl.² B60K 9/00
[52] U.S. Cl. .... 280/87.04 A; 280/11.1 BR; D21/227
[58] Field of Search .... 280/87.04 A, 87.04 R, 280/11.1 BR, 11.1 BT, 11.2, 767; D34/15 AT, 15 AJ

[56] **References Cited**
U.S. PATENT DOCUMENTS

D. 244,706	6/1977	Vela	280/87.04 A
2,608,430	8/1952	Robert	280/767 X
3,310,320	3/1967	Hanna et al.	280/87.04 A
3,379,454	4/1968	Woodman	280/87.04 A

FOREIGN PATENT DOCUMENTS

494195 3/1930 Fed. Rep. of Germany .. 280/11.1 BR
1121516 1/1962 Fed. Rep. of Germany .. 280/11.1 BR

Primary Examiner—John A. Pekar
Attorney, Agent, or Firm—Fulwider, Patton, Rieber, Lee & Utecht

[57] **ABSTRACT**

There is disclosed a skateboard pivot roller assembly including a mounting bracket formed with a generally flat upwardly facing mounting surface for mating with the flat underside of the skateboard platform and is formed in one extremity with a roller housing including a downwardly opening ball socket having a rotatable ball mounted therein and projecting downwardly therefrom to have its lower spherical surface spaced somewhat above the plane of the bottoms of the skateboard wheels. Thus, the skateboard rider can shift his weight to the end of the skateboard having such assembly mounted thereunderneath to tilt the skateboard thus lowering such bracket to engage the pivot ball with the ground to enable pivoting and maneuvering of the rider with at least a portion of his weight carried on such ball.

10 Claims, 7 Drawing Figures

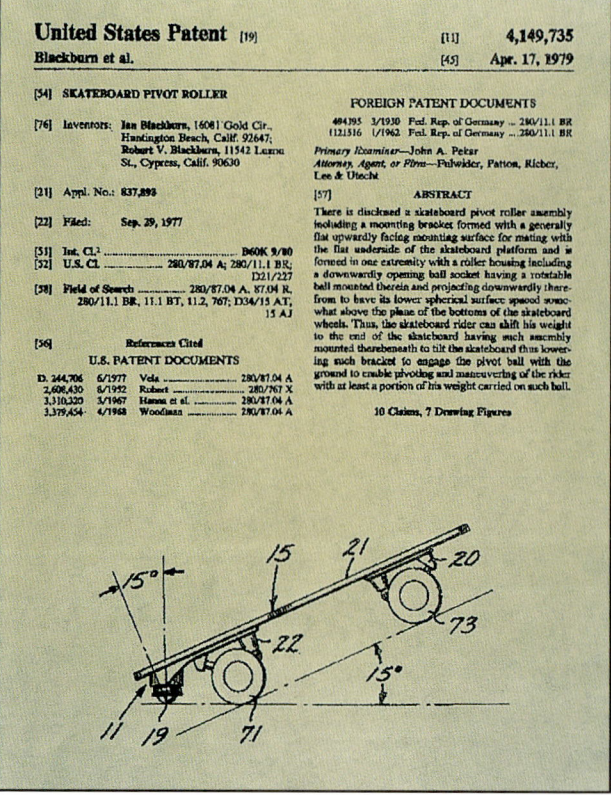

United States Patent [19]

Roden

[11] **4,062,557**

[45] Dec. 13, 1977

[54] **EIGHT WHEEL SKATEBOARD**

[76] Inventor: Harry F. Roden, 3863 Merle Ave., Culver City, Calif. 90230

[21] Appl. No.: 715,877

[22] Filed: Aug. 19, 1976

[51] Int. Cl.² A63C 17/00
[52] U.S. Cl. .... 280/87.04 A; 280/11.27
[58] Field of Search .... 280/87.04 A, 87.04 R, 280/11.1 BT, 11.28, 11.27, 11.19

[56] References Cited

U.S. PATENT DOCUMENTS

1,247,801	11/1917	Eggs	280/87.04 A
2,581,809	1/1952	Murray	280/11.28

Primary Examiner—Joseph F. Peters, Jr.
Assistant Examiner—John A. Pekar
Attorney, Agent, or Firm—Ralph B. Pastoriza

[57] **ABSTRACT**

A skateboard has front and rear trucks each supporting four wheels centrally pivoted to the axle on the undercarriages of the skateboard normally provided for the conventional type front and rear wheels. Each truck can rock about its central pivot on the axis and thereby reduce the amplitude of small bumps experienced by the board successively passed over by the leading and trailing wheels of each truck.

3 Claims, 3 Drawing Figures

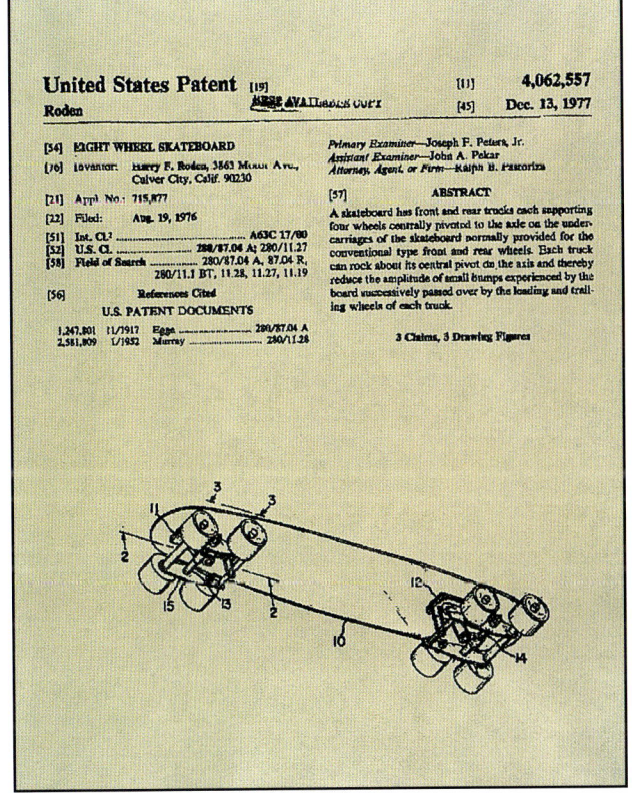

United States Patent [19]

Cohen

[11] **4,095,817**

[45] Jun. 20, 1978

[54] **WHEELIE SKATEBOARD**

[75] Inventor: Daniel R. Cohen, Port Washington, N.Y.

[73] Assignee: Gustave Miller, Miami, Fla.

[21] Appl. No.: 713,676

[22] Filed: Aug. 12, 1976

[51] Int. Cl.² A63C 17/04
[52] U.S. Cl. .... 280/87.04 A
[58] Field of Search .... 280/87.04 A, 87.04 R, 280/11.2, 11.1 BT, 11.1 R, 11.28, 11.27; D34/15 AJ; 272/70, 96

[56] References Cited

U.S. PATENT DOCUMENTS

D. 212,105	8/1968	Persinger et al.	D34/15 AJ
2,253,012	8/1941	Benner et al.	280/11.1 BT
2,427,572	9/1947	Pharns	280/11.19
3,399,904	9/1968	Schinke	280/87.04 A
3,442,528	5/1969	Rademacher	280/87.04 A
3,565,454	2/1971	Stevenson	280/87.04 A
3,630,540	12/1971	Smith	280/87.04 A

3,990,713	11/1976	Hokanson	280/87.04 A
4,040,639	8/1977	Scardenzan	280/87.04 A

FOREIGN PATENT DOCUMENTS

1,215,053	4/1960	France	280/87.04 A
616,723	1/1949	United Kingdom	280/87.04 A

OTHER PUBLICATIONS

Playthings, 2/1976, Toy Fair Edition, p. 184.

Primary Examiner—David M. Mitchell
Attorney, Agent, or Firm—Gustave Miller

[57] **ABSTRACT**

This device is a wheelie skateboard and consists of a more or less conventional skateboard to which is added a rearward upwardly inclined kicktail. Conventional skateboard wheels are mounted on the bottom of the conventional skateboard section. In this device, a third pair of wheels are mounted on the bottom of the inclined kicktail section.

1 Claim, 4 Drawing Figures

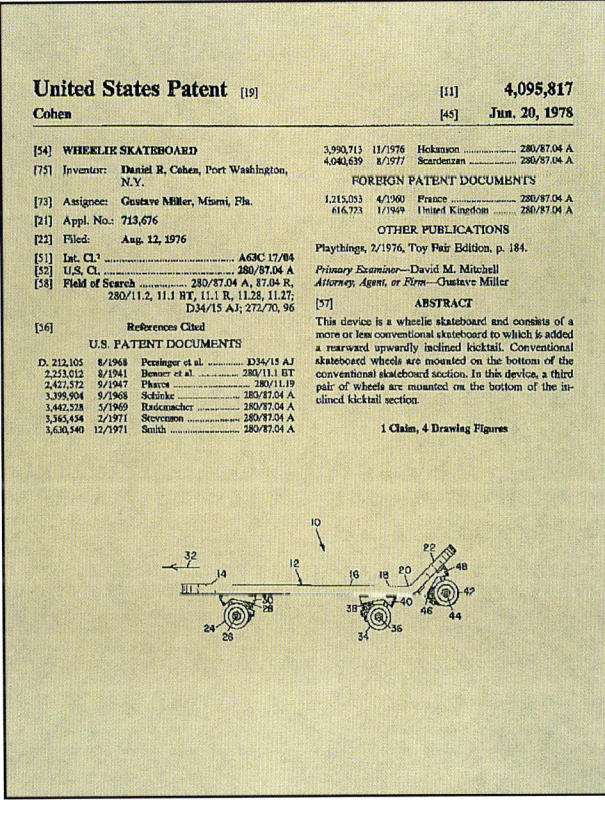

United States Patent [19]

Scardenzan

[11] **4,040,639**

[45] Aug. 9, 1977

[54] **SKATEBOARD**

[76] Inventor: Anthony Scardenzan, 269 N. Hillcrest Blvd., Inglewood, Calif. 90301

[21] Appl. No.: 670,361

[22] Filed: Mar. 25, 1976

[51] Int. Cl.² A63C 17/14
[52] U.S. Cl. .... 280/87.04 A; D34/15 AJ
[58] Field of Search .... 280/87.04 A, 87.04 R, 280/87.01, 11.2, 11.22, 637; D34/15 AT, 15 AJ

[56] References Cited

U.S. PATENT DOCUMENTS

2,198,667	4/1940	Hughes	280/87.04 A
2,631,861	3/1953	Daniska	280/11.2
3,235,282	2/1966	Bostick	280/87.04 A
3,288,251	11/1966	Sakawa	188/29

3,565,450	2/1971	Rosenthal	280/637
3,565,454	2/1971	Stevenson	280/87.04 A
3,622,172	11/1971	Goodwin	280/11.22 X
3,990,713	11/1976	Hokanson	280/11.2 X
D. 200,864	4/1965	de Roco	280/87.04 A

Primary Examiner—Joseph F. Peters, Jr.
Assistant Examiner—John A. Pekar
Attorney, Agent, or Firm—Keith D. Beecher

[57] **ABSTRACT**

A skateboard is provided which is constructed to incorporate a braking device at its rear end for safety purposes; and which also includes in the embodiment to be described, a line tethered to the forward end which may be grasped by the operator, and a foot binding as additional safety features.

2 Claims, 6 Drawing Figures

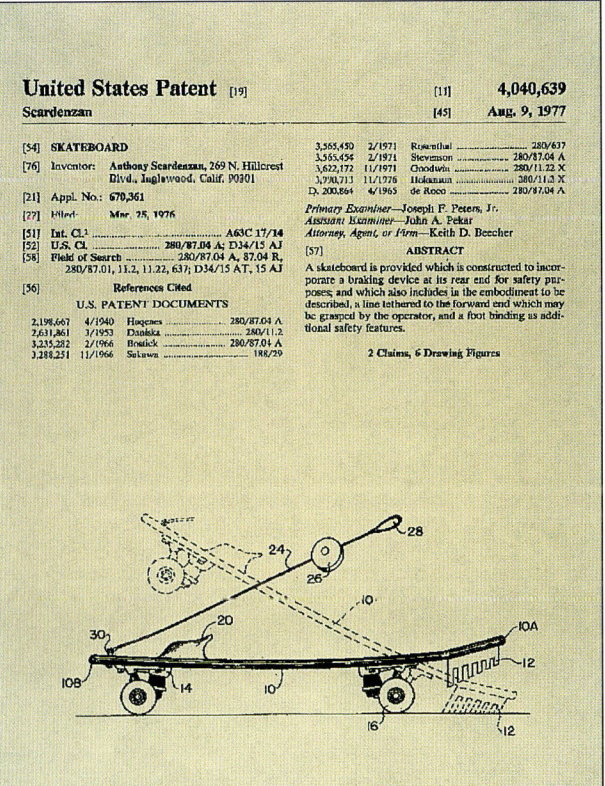

• 1938: nuclear fission was conceived and work on the atomic bomb began.

• 1938: Minimum wage was 25 cents an hour.

• 1939: Television was introduced into our society and World War II started.

Roller Derby was popularized in 1935 in roller rinks, bringing new popularity to roller skating. 1941 saw new wheel patents. In 1943 the Ware brothers patented wheels and trucks; they founded the company we know as Chicago. The United States had just come out of the bleak years of the Depression, and times were still tough. The only "skateboard" obtainable by the average kid was made of broken roller skates strapped and nailed to a board. Basically, anything with wheels was utilized.

I personally tried to recreate an early 2 x 4 skateboard. With a pair of roller skates from the 1920s I went to work. This skate was very easy to separate from itself; by taking one small nut off, I could slide them apart. The front key mechanism could turn all the way open and I could coax it into fitting a 2 x 4. With the key it could probably be cinched quite tight, even utilizing the leather strap over the top of the 2 x 4. With a couple of carefully-placed nails and screws, you would be motivated for glide!

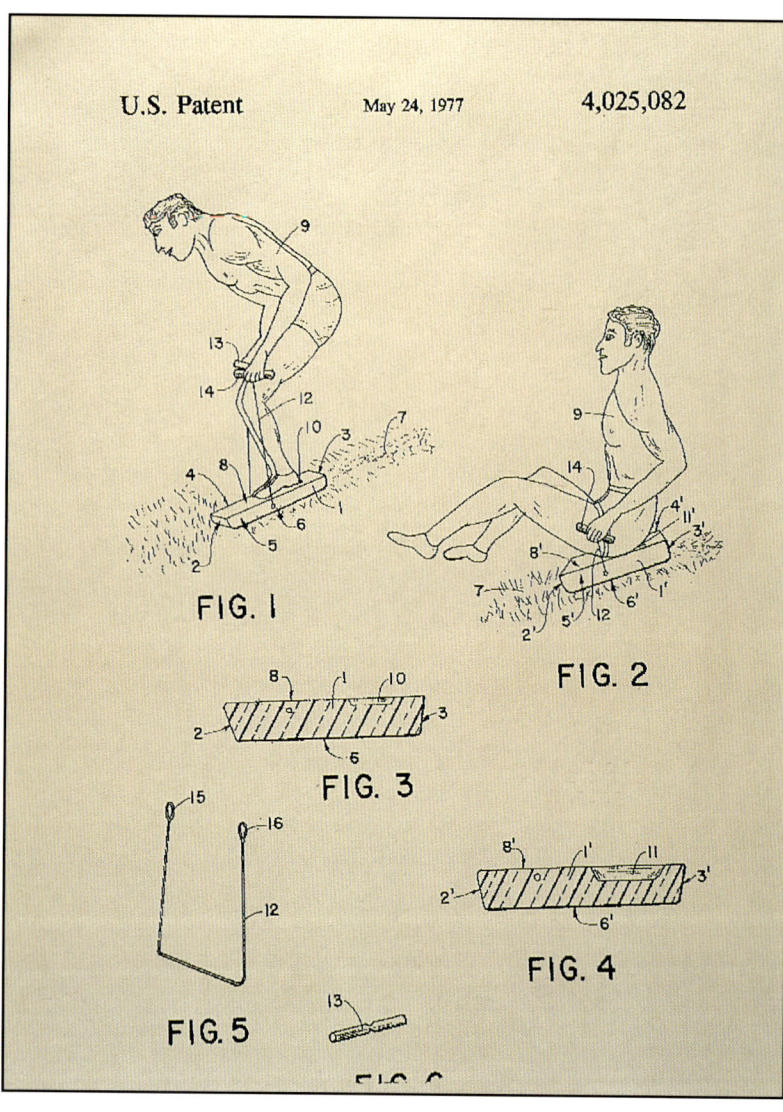

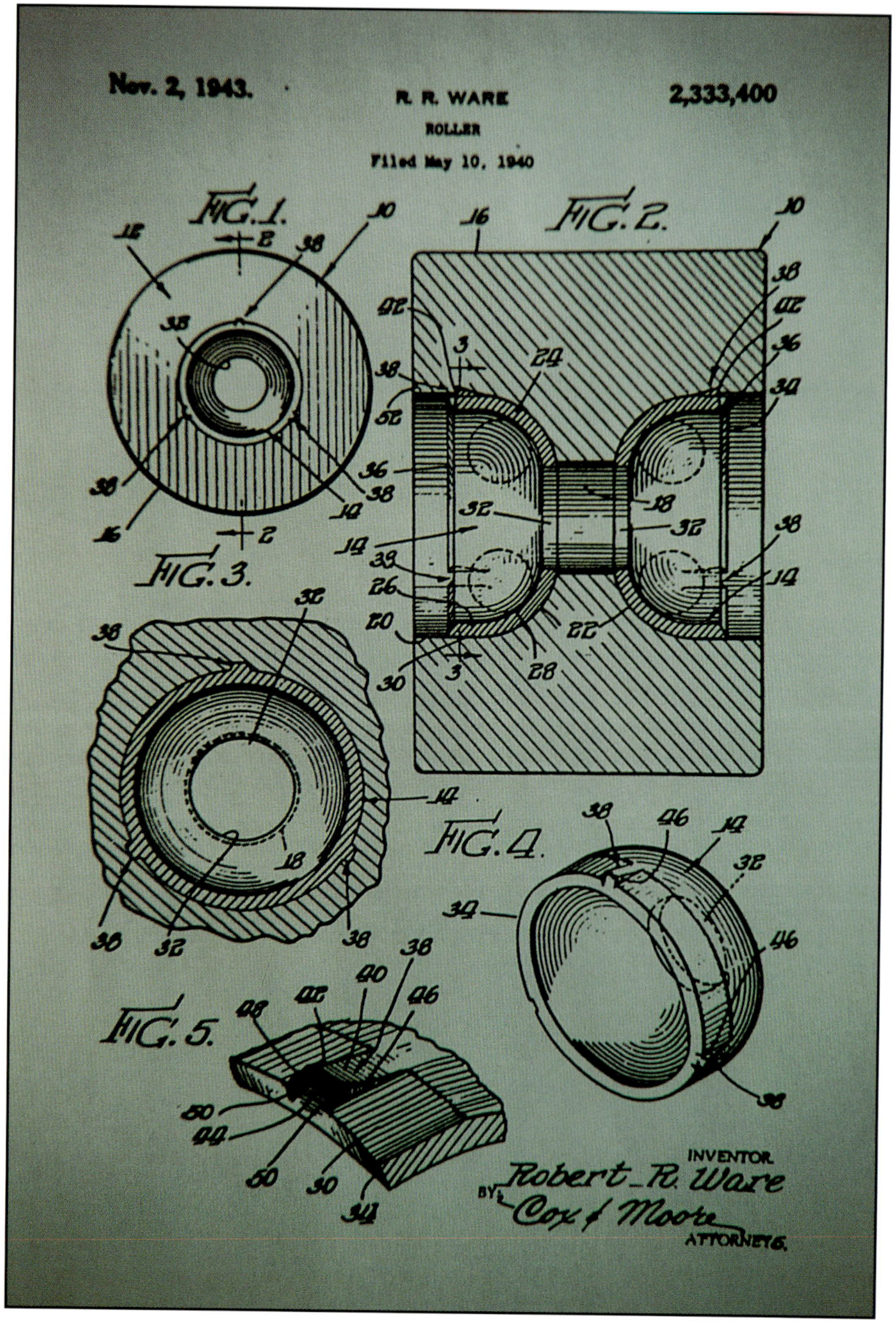

Patent drawing by Robert R. Ware, one of the Ware brothers. Chicago Wheel held patents on open ball-bearing wheels in 1943. *Courtesy Dale Smith*

• 1945: World War Two ended. Hitler committed suicide.

The world had been locked in conflict for the first half of this decade, and now toys could be considered again. The United Kingdom was into wheeled coasters in 1949.

Chapter 2

1950-1960

As I come closer to uncovering the next bit of tantalizing information the big picture becomes clearer. First there were ice skates, then wheels were put on them. Before long the wheels were taken off skates and put on boards with fruit or soap boxes and handles. Warren Bolster remembers kids using these scooters in New York City in the 1950s. The scooters were primarily used as transportation, but no kid could miss the fun of getting their kicks from them. Finally they lost their boxes and kids started to ride them with both feet and no hands. These first skateboards were made of 2 x 4s, old planks, or anything else that you could stand on.

Union Flyer by Brunswick Sports, steel wheels. *Courtesy Todd Huber.* $600-800

Perfect examples of early roller skate scooters. These scooters would make any collector's mouth water. *Courtesy Todd Huber.*

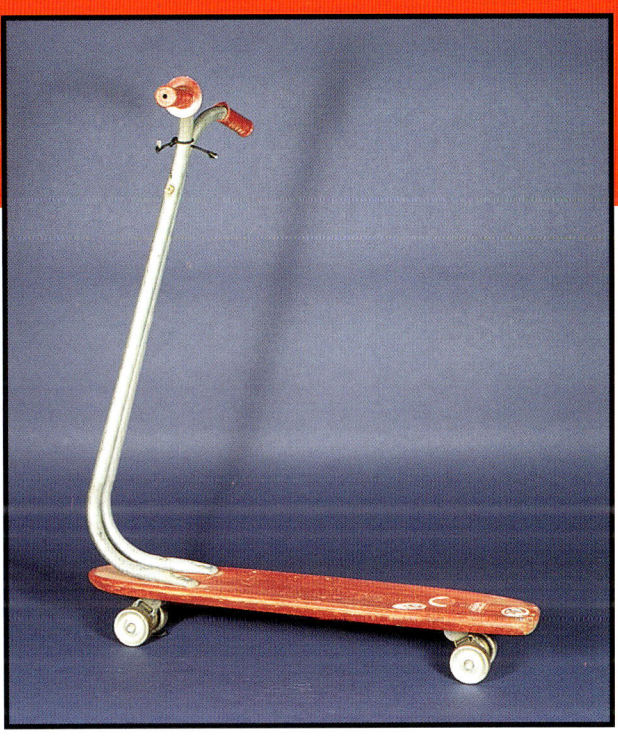

Earliest roller skate scooter with accessories. Painted-on skull and crossbones, a fin for stability, and even an early logo. $50-100 *Courtesy Jim O'Mahoney. Photo: Rhyn Noll.*

A Red Rascal with handlebars you could actually steer, steel wheels, and rubber patch for grip. *Courtesy Todd Huber.* $600-800

An early Nash scooter with steel wheels. *Courtesy Todd Huber.* $600-800

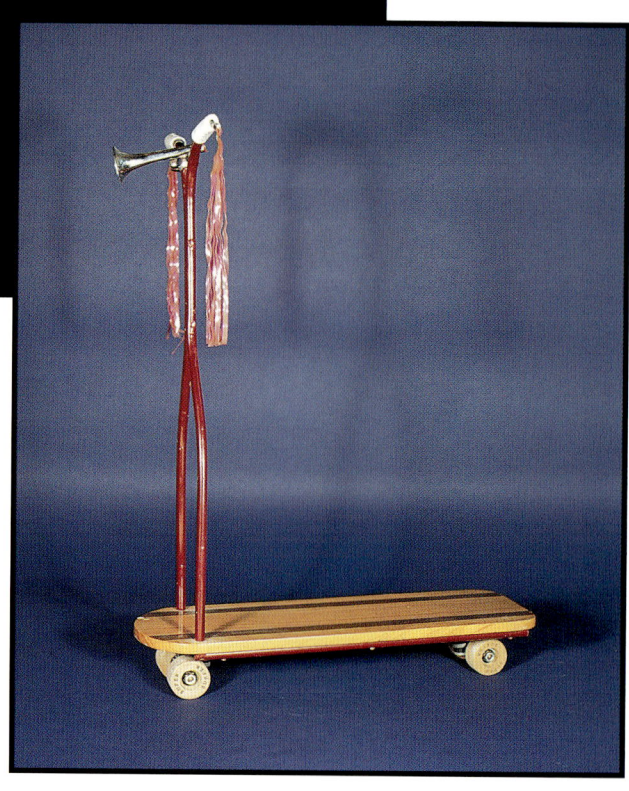

Torpedo Scooter from O'Conner Industries, Detroit, Michigan, with single steel wheel in front. *Courtesy Todd Huber.* $600-800

Wooden Scooter with steel wheels, said to have come from the circus. *Courtesy Todd Huber.* $800-1000

Junior grip with horn, laminated deck, and super stoker clay wheels. *Courtesy Todd Huber.* $600-800

The Fifties was the golden era of surfing and the sport of riding a board with wheels was made popular by a group of surf kids in southern California, like Pete Perkins from Wind & Sea and Denny and Kemp Aaberg. These guys were young surfers who were riding skateboards in the fifties. Surfboard manufacturers of the day took notice and started to build the first skateboards for the public. These boards were 2 x 4s or plywood—anything for a platform—with crude steel wheels taken from a roller skate. The wheels were nailed or screwed onto the board. Comfort was not an issue. The type and style of board riding were simple and straightforward.

Pat and Mike O'Niell, brothers on an early boardskate. *Courtesy Jack O'Niell*

Tom Craig and his brother on what looks to be a pallet with wheels. *Courtesy Tom Craig.*

Not too many photos exist of roller skate scooters. Here is one Jim O'Mahoney snapped. He had amazing foresight. *Courtesy Jim O'Mahoney.*

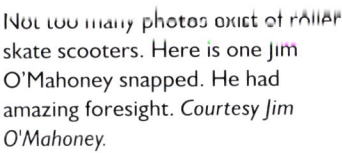

I hear tales of Mr. Carl Jensen in the late Fifties, a man who built early skateboards and brought them into my dad's shop, Greg Noll Surfboards. Greg recalls Mr. Jensen as the first to sell skateboards to his Hermosa Beach shop in 1958, and considers him a founder of the commercial skateboard. Included was a Greg Noll surfboard logo with rubber-stamp style graphics on the primitive board. Greg's main focus was on surfboards, but this early date could mean that his shop may have been the earliest retailer of skateboards. Greg Noll skateboards are rare, but they do exist today. Dale Smith has been offered $5,000 for his.

Greg also recalls that Dewey Weber and Hobie Alter were early believers and promoters, selling the bulk of skateboards in these pre-boom days.

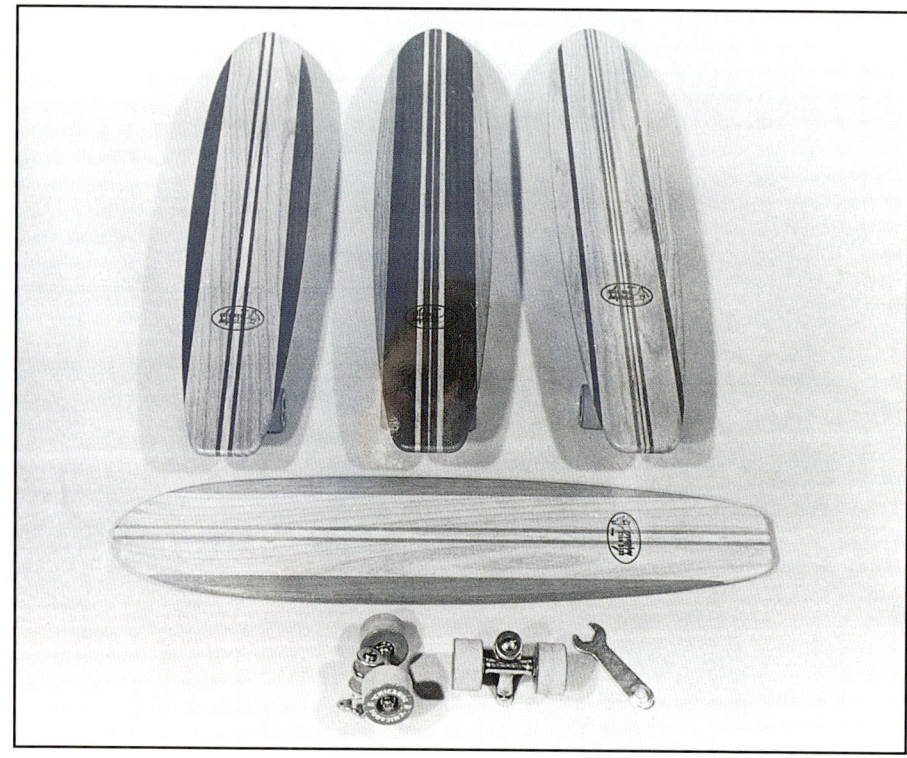

This is one of the oldest known advertisements in the skateboarding world. They were called "Bun Boards," because when you fell, you fell on your bun! These publications were printed in 1961; today they are probably worth about $300 each. This is Rick Griffin's earliest commercial artwork—he was one of the first artists for the skateboarding world. *Courtesy and ©Greg Noll Surfboards.*

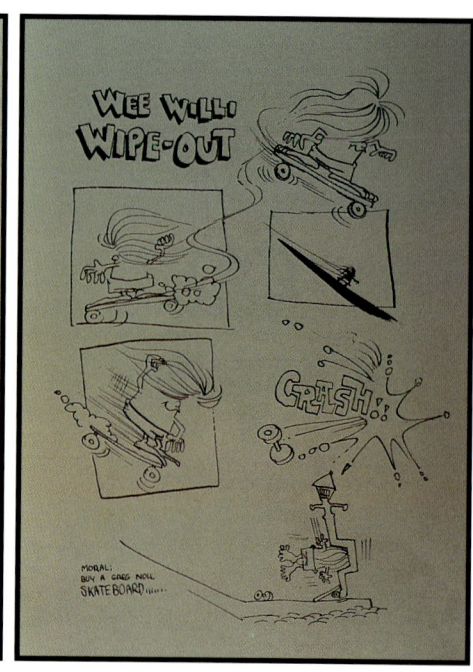

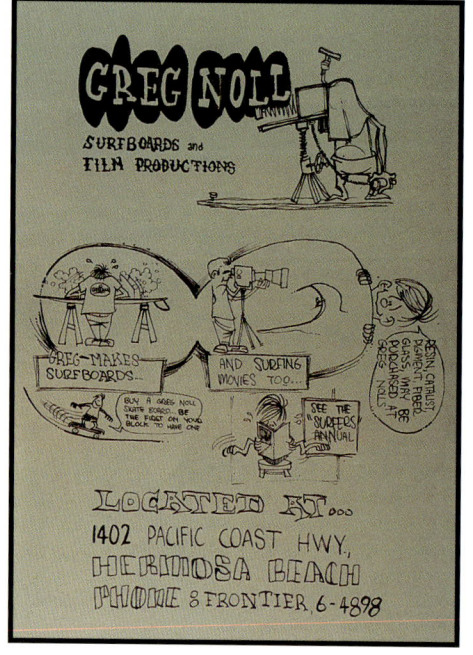

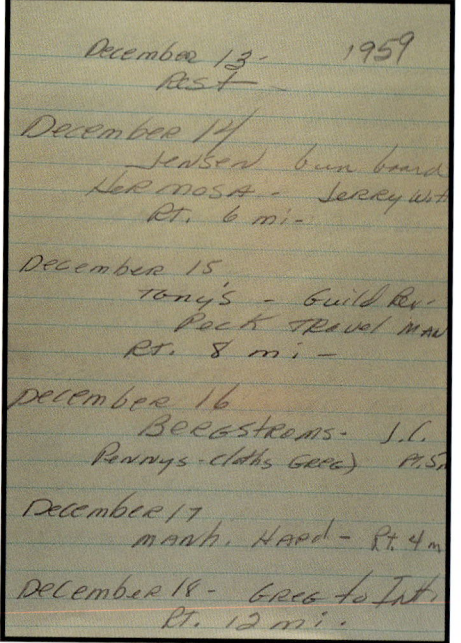

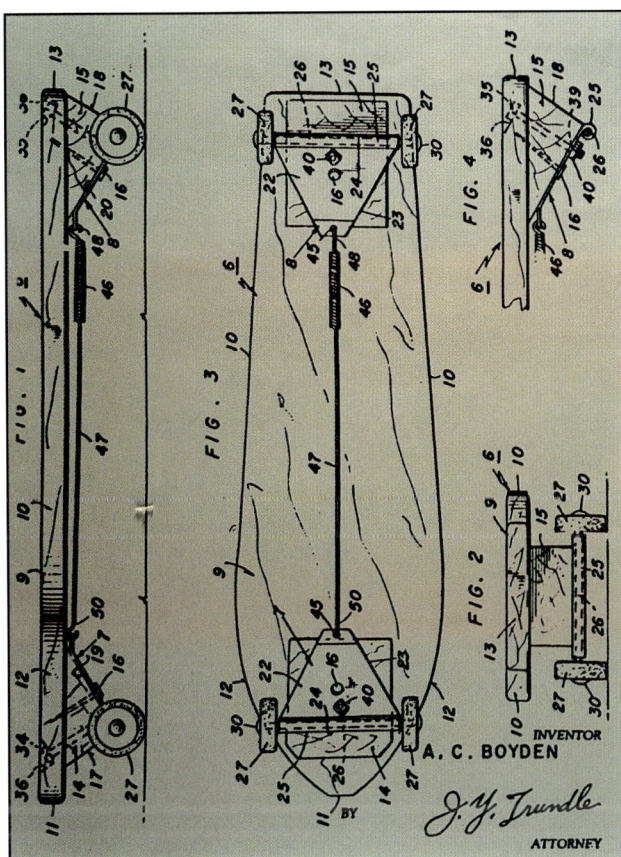

Early Humco patent. *Courtesy Dale Smith.*

In 1958m A. C. Boyden, better known as Humco, patented one of the earliest recognizable skateboards. In 1959 a complete skateboard was manufactured in Litchfield, Illinois by a company called Roller Derby. It could be bought for under five dollars. In Malibu Beach, the movie *Gidget* was just about to come on the scene, spreading the romance and popularity of surfing and skating to an even wider audience. The general consensus was skateboarding, or "sidewalk surfing," was a good way for surfers to cruise out the flat spells.

• 1960: JFK was elected president.

The skateboard quickly moved from the beaches to the cities as urban kids eagerly adopted the sport. Commercial boards were just coming on the scene, so the average kid was still kyping his sister's skates to nail to a 2 x 4 deck; wood composite roller skate wheels began to take the place of steel wheels, to be followed by clay.

Baton twirler throwing her hands up in glee, riding a skateboard. *Courtesy Todd Huber.*

But surf companies and individual entrepreneurs began to see the business possibilities in the skateboard. In 1962 Val Surf, owned by Bill Richards and his sons, Mark and Kurt, was one of the earliest retail stores to sell complete decks. Hobie Alter credits Larry Stevenson with the first production skateboard. At first, Hobie made a laminated wood board, Larry produced a solid board, and with it the era of production-oriented skateboards begins. Stevenson started Makaha Skateboards in 1963, and introduced design and marketing innovations that still influence the sport.

The first companies to manufacture skateboards in high numbers were Makaha, Hobie, Nash, McGregor, and Vita Pakt. The early decks were made in oak, ash, and mahogany. The first production trucks were made by Chicago, Sure Grip, and Roller Derby. Private labels were Hobie, Makaha, Leisure Line and Sport Fun. In 1963, the first skateboard competition was held in Hermosa Beach, California at Pier Avenue Junior High School. First place went to Brad "Squeak" Blank, who won overall.

These early companies may not have invented the skateboard, but they are responsible for the first stoke, and in manufacturing and producing the first affordable skateboards. When you look at today's skateboard and trace its family tree, you will find that these are some of its fathers—the Richards, Larry Stevenson, A.C. Boyden, Ware brothers, Carl Jensen, Greg Noll, Dewey Weber, the Aabergs, Peter Perkins, and Hobie Alter. Skateboarding grew slowly until 1964.

Mark Richards, one of the earliest retailers, throwing a nice kick turn down. *Courtesy Leroy Grannis.*

Tommy Ryan riding what looks to be freshly poured concrete. Rides were rough in the 1960s! If you have ever ridden a set of clay or steel wheels, you know. *Courtesy Classic Stoner Photos.*

• 1964: Martin Luther King won the Nobel Peace Prize.

In 1964 Hobie licensed his name to Vida Pakt, and mass-production of the skateboard arrived. Hobie tells of a time when orders came in faster than the new company could meet them.

The first promotional bus trip was taken in 1964 by the Hobie Team, who traveled to the East Coast and back. Bruce Logan won the International Surf Festival in Hermosa Beach, California. Skaters were emulating surf moves, hanging ten, carving cutback, and nose riding. The media stars were Tommy Lee Ryan, Mickey Maga, Dave and Steve Hilton, Torger Johnson, Danny Bearer, Danny Schaeffer and Joey Cabell.

The 1960s were the golden era of skateboard manufacturing, and people and companies took notice. In three years, over 50,000,000 boards were sold when Vida Pakt entered the scene, and overproduction created a glut in the market. It drove the cost down—good for consumer, bad for small-company manufacturers.

That same year *Skater Dater,* an 18 minute short film, was produced. It won the Academy Award for Best Short Film, and added to the evidence that skateboarding had become a full-fledged fad.

Jacks skate team. 1965 Performing some of the cutting edge tricks of the 1960s. *Courtesy Classic Stoner Photos.*

1965 Hobie team photo. Note the early grip tape. *Courtesy Classic Stoner Photos.*

Jacks team, 1965. There is something about early Stoner photographs that capture the moment and the feel of a time in culture. *Courtesy Classic Stoner Photos.*

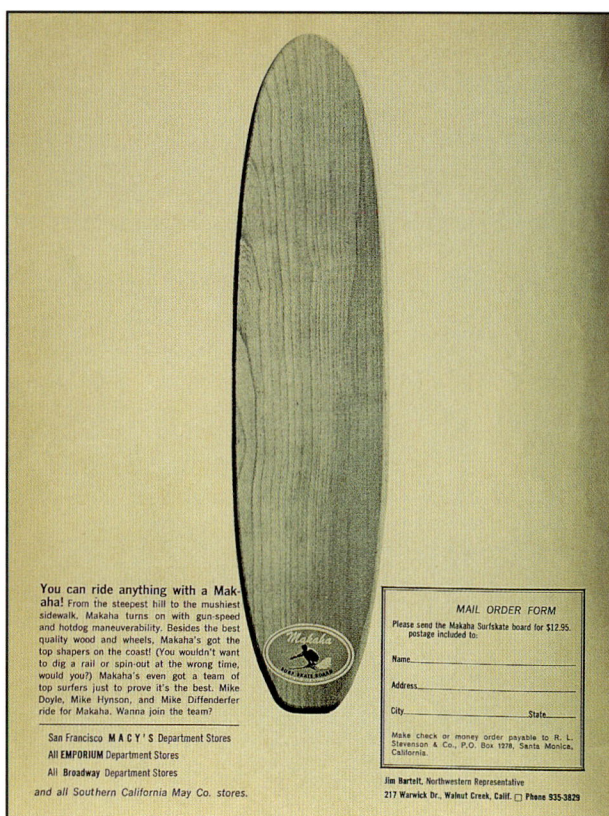

Classic early skate ads from *Surfing Illustrated*. One featuring Mike Hynson, surf star, posing for Makaha ads. Courtesy Roger Graves.

Memorabilia from earliest competition in Hermosa Beach, California. *Courtesy Tom Craig. Photo: Rhyn Noll* $20-50

Ultimate by Sports Fun, pressed core, fiber resin, molded rocker, 29 inches long. *Courtesy Ed Economy.* $300-500

LEFT: Rolla-Board Rocket, from Great Britain by Union, rubber wheels and plywood, 29 inches long. *Courtesy Ed Economy.* $500-600

RIGHT: Roll n Surf, solid wood with a unique rubber stopper at the tail, steel wheels, 24 inches long. *Courtesy Ed Economy.* $200-300

LEFT to RIGHT:

Apollo Skate, solid core made in Little Rock Arkansas. Steel wheels, 23 inches long. Part of a group of space flight skateboards; the other two are Atlas and Saturn. $500-600

Sidewalk Surfboard by Nash, Catalina, clay wheels and one of the best examples of early Longboard, very rare, 44 inches long, $3000-5000

Hang Five, clay wheels, 19 inches long. $200-300

Mustang, by Duro. $200-250

Courtesy Todd Huber.

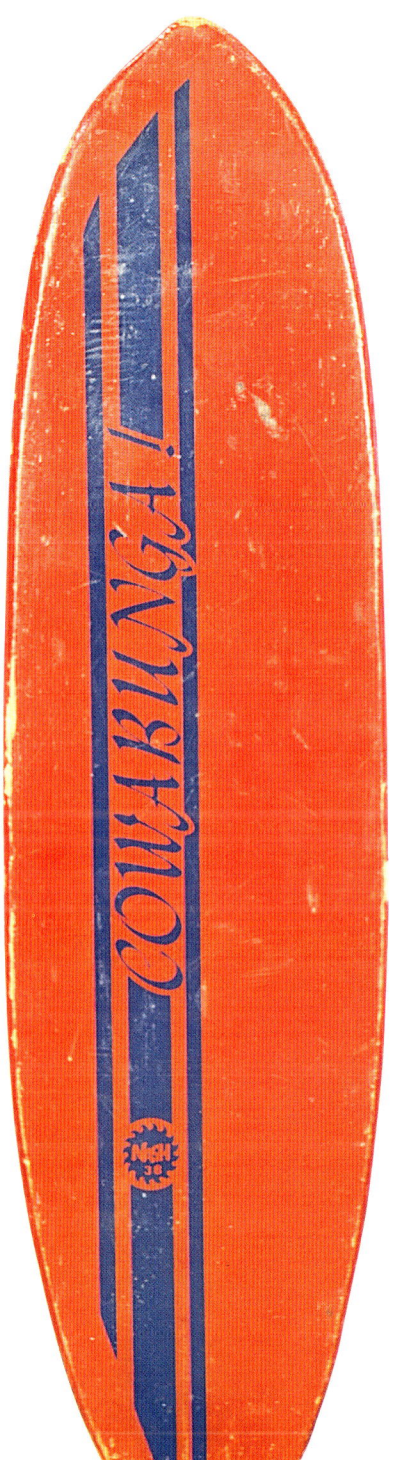

LEFT to RIGHT:

Saturn, one of a group of space boards. $150-250

Hawaiian Surf with Union hardware, 28" long, $200-400.

Sidewalk surfboard, Malibu, by Champion. 36" long. $800-1500.

Cowabunga, by Nash. 22" long. $200-300.

Courtesy Todd Huber.

PRODUCT PHOTOS FROM 1960s:

The Indy 500, 29" long. $150-200. *Courtesy Todd Huber.*

Bottom view of Fifteen Toes, by Nash. *Courtesy Todd Huber.*

Fifteen Toes, by Nash. *Courtesy Todd Huber.* $150-200

Tuck and Roll, by Ray Brown Automotive. It came in five colors in the 1960s and cost $15.95. *Courtesy Todd Huber.* $500-800.

Tenderfoot, by Nash. *Courtesy Todd Huber.* $150-200

Mustang, by Roller Derby. *Courtesy Todd Huber.* $150-200

Deluxe, by Roller Derby. *Courtesy Todd Huber.* $150-200

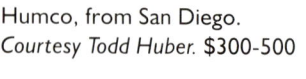

Humco, from San Diego. *Courtesy Todd Huber.* $300-500

LEFT: This board is from New Zealand. *Courtesy Todd Huber.* $300-500

RIGHT: Bottom of the board from New Zealand.

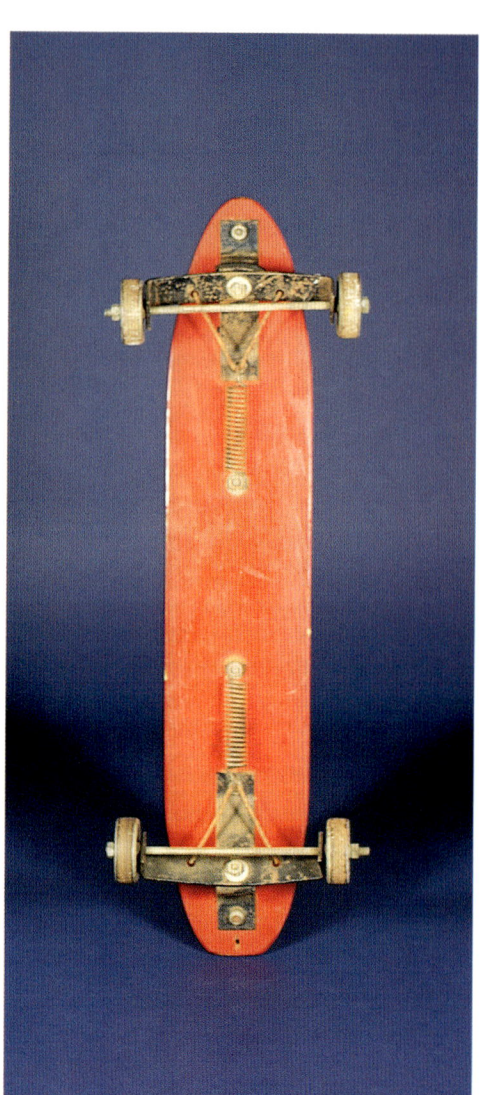

Bottom of Humco.

Humco. *Courtesy Todd Huber.*
$300-400

Bottom of Humco.

Surfa Sam, from Australia. Very
rare. *Courtesy Todd Huber.* $500-800

The Skid-ooo, 36" long. *Courtesy Todd Huber.* $800-1500

Super Surfer from Santa Monica, California. Fiberglass construction, molded rocker, textured deck, clay wheels, 27 inches long. *Courtesy of Ed Economy.* $500-600

Sears Hang Ten with clay wheels, 35 inches long. *Courtesy Ed Economy.* $400-500

Sidewalk Surfboard by Nash, with laminated hardwoods, clay wheels. 26 inches long. *Courtesy Ed Economy.* $200-300

Road Surfer by Moen, steel wheels, 24 inches long. *Courtesy Ed Economy.* $200-300

Rinky Dink, solid wood construction, steel wheels. *Courtesy Ed Economy.* $200-300

Big Wheeler, by Adolf Kefer, Norfield, Illinois. 29 inches, clay Chicago wheels. *Courtesy Ed Economy.* $200-300

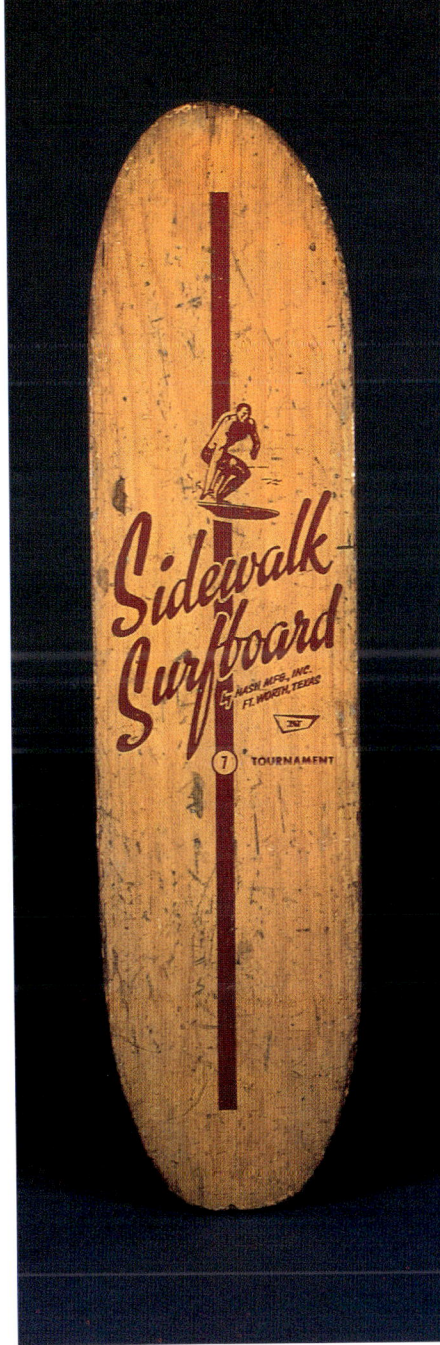

Sidewalk Surfboard by Nash in Fort Worth, Texas, steel wheels, 24 inches long. *Courtesy Ed Economy.* $300-500

Hedlund, clay wheels, solid wood core, 21 inches long. *Courtesy Ed Economy.* $200-300

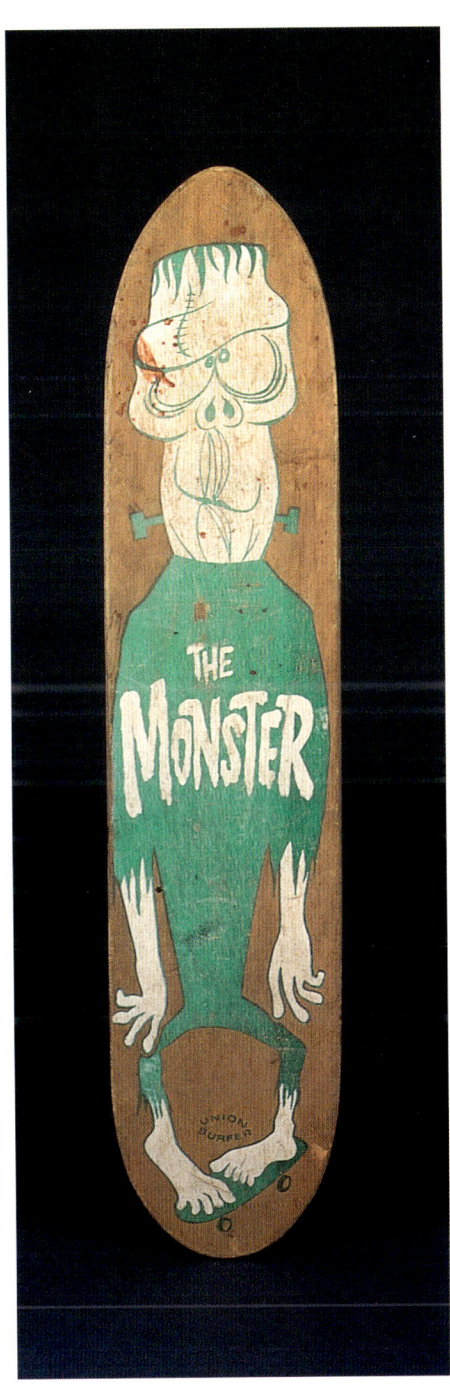

Monster by Union, Torrington, Connecticut. Hard rubber wheels, 23 inches long. *Courtesy Ed Economy.* $500-600

Roll Surf by Midonn, winged roller skate graphics depicting transition from roller skate to skateboard. Rubber wheels, 22 inches long. *Courtesy Ed Economy.* $300-400

A laminated hardwood board by Sincor, clay wheels, 21 inches long. *Courtesy Ed Economy.* $150-200

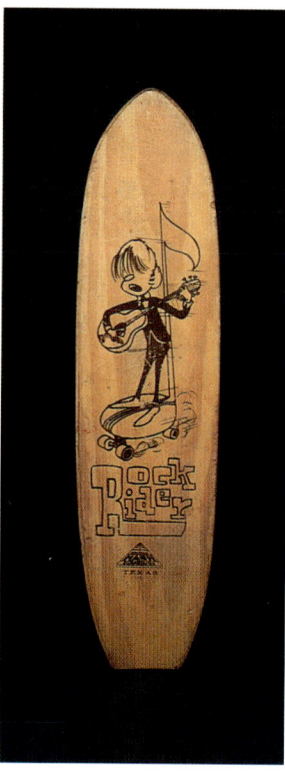

Nash Rock Rider, a possible takeoff from the Beatles craze. Plastic wheels, 21 inches long. *Courtesy Ed Economy.* $200-300

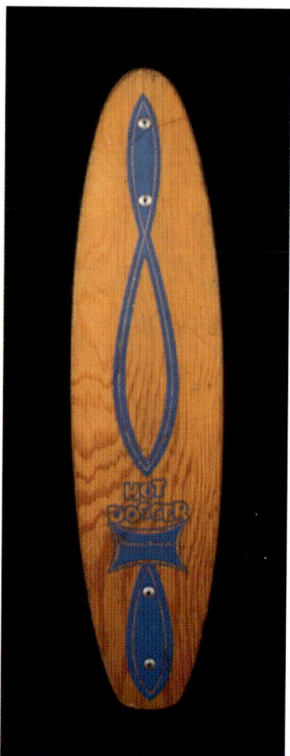

Hot Dogger, 5-ply core, unique double rivet design, steel wheels, built in Torrance, California. 24 inches long. *Courtesy Ed Economy.* $300-400

Jacks Surf Shop, clay wheels. The set is $50-80. *Courtesy Ed and Allen Economy.*

San Diegan by Humco, solid birch, sure grip clay wheels, 23 inches long. $300-400

Classic "Say Hey Willie Mays" model with a story that can't be repeated. Clay wheels, 5-ply construction by Union Surfer. $2000-3000

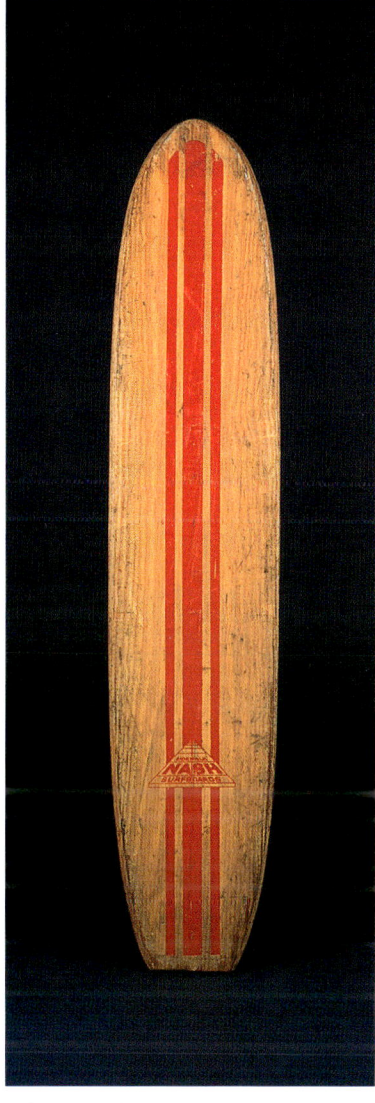

Fliback Skate Racer with #11, Ned Jarred's racing number. Made in North Carolina, 26 inches long. *Courtesy Ed Economy.* $500-600

Sport Flight by Sears, Chicago clay wheels, 23 inches long. *Courtesy Ed Economy.* $300-400

Val Surf Logo with a Hobie deck, clay wheels, and early grip tape, 30 inches long. *Courtesy Ed Economy.* $500-1000, depending on condition.

Duke Kahanamoku, clay wheels, 29 inches, super blue graphics, great portrait of the Duke *Courtesy Ed Economy.* $1500-2000

Sidewalk Surfboard by Nash, clay wheels, 27 inches long. *Courtesy Ed Economy.* $200-300

Con, solid core, sure grip clay wheels, very rare, 26 inches long. *Courtesy Ed Economy.* $900-1000

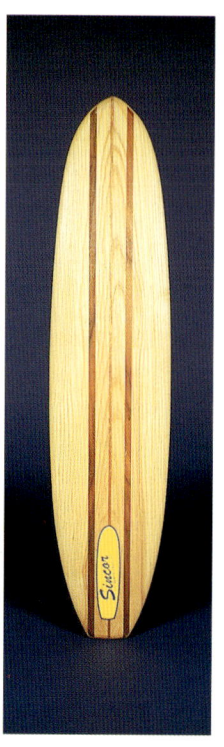

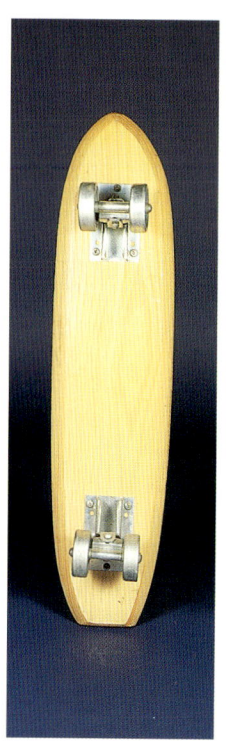

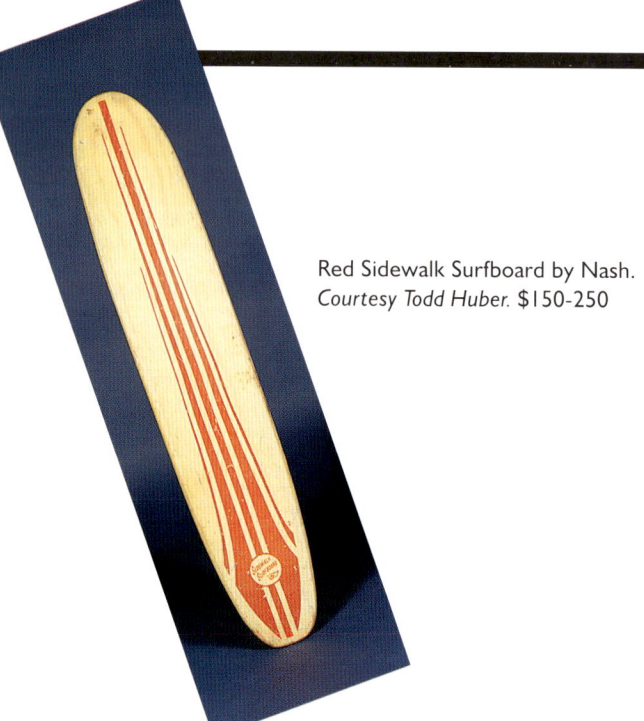

Red Sidewalk Surfboard by Nash.
Courtesy Todd Huber. $150-250

FROM LEFT to RIGHT:

The Black Knight. Late model, clay wheels. *Courtesy Todd Huber.* $75-125

AerFlyte by Roller Derby. *Courtesy Todd Huber.* $200-250

Sincor, out of Venice, California. *Courtesy Todd Huber.* $200-250

Red Shark, by Nash. Came in different colors. *Courtesy Todd Huber.* $75-125

Bottom view of Red Shark

Wakiki Sidewalk Surfboard by Champion. *Courtesy Todd Huber.* $500-800

Sidewalk Surfer. *Courtesy Todd Huber.* $300-400

Blue Sidewalk Surfboard by Nash. *Courtesy Todd Huber.* $150-250

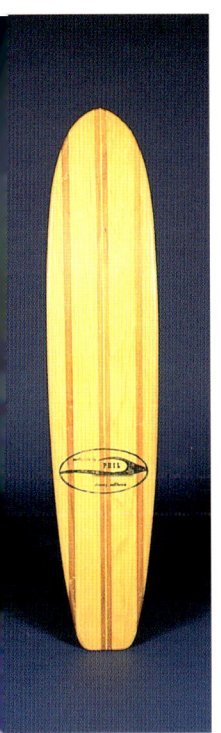 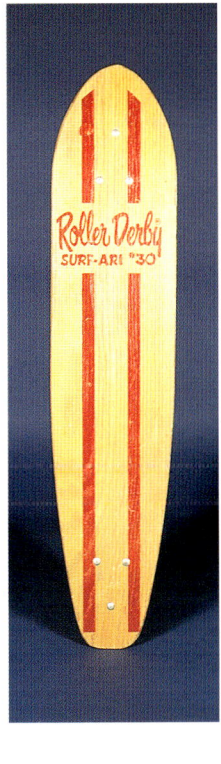  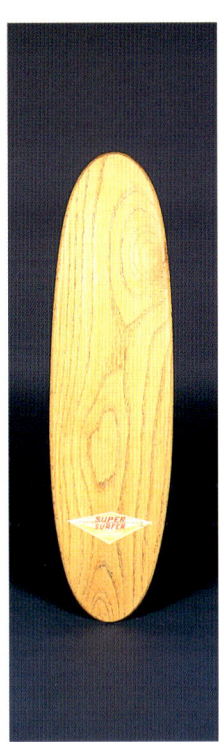 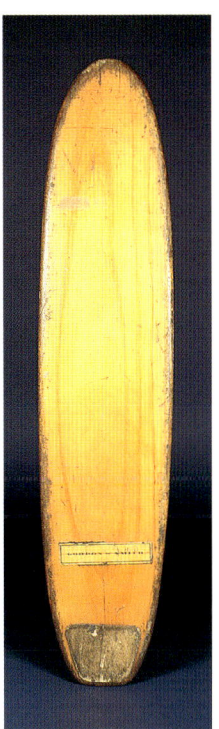  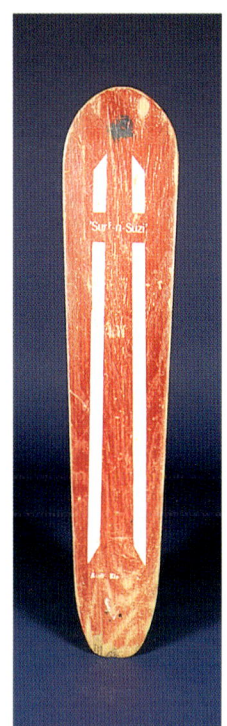 

FROM LEFT to RIGHT:

Skateboards by Phil. *Courtesy Todd Huber.* $100-200

Surf-ari #30 by Roller Derby. *Courtesy Todd Huber.* $200-275

Hot Dogger by P.F. *Courtesy Todd Huber.* $250-250

Super Surfer. *Courtesy Todd Huber.* $150-200

Gordon-n-Smith early grip pad. *Courtesy Todd Huber.* $300-400

Bun Buster by Cooley. *Courtesy Todd Huber.* $175-300

Surf-n-Suzi. *Courtesy Todd Huber.* $175-300

Zipees Sidewalk Surfboard. *Courtesy Todd Huber.* $150-250

Official Skee-skate by Tresco.
Courtesy Todd Huber. $100-150

Early steel wheel. *Courtesy Todd Huber.*

One of the first real longboards, Koa Birch, 44-inch Royal Hawaiian. *Courtesy Ed Economy.* $5000

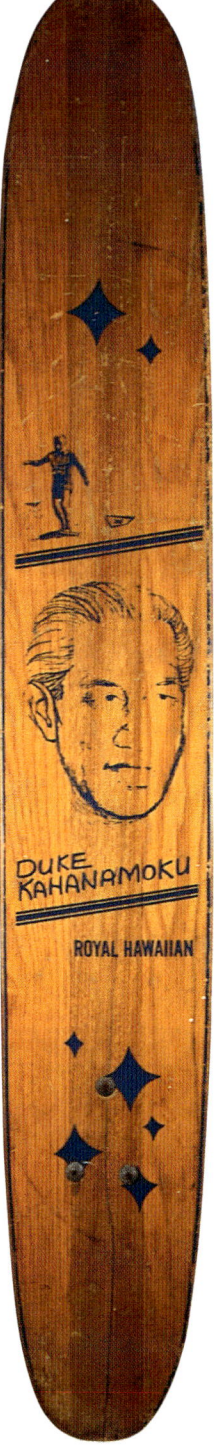

Makaha Commander, the longest board Makaha made. Laminated hardwood, 33 inches long, clay wheels. *Courtesy Ed Economy.* $1000-1500

Marge Calhoun and her daughters Robin and Candy skate down a bike path in southern California. *Courtesy Leroy Grannis*

Side Walk Surfboard by Nash, 22 inches long, steel wheels. *Courtesy Ed Economy.* $150-200

Fliback Skate Racer #43, race car driver Richard Petty's number. Made in Highpoint, North Carolina. Steel wheels, 21 inches long. *Courtesy Ed Economy.* $300-500

Sidewalk Surfboard with an early roller skate truck and clay wheels, made from mahogany by Nash. 34 inches long. *Courtesy Ed Economy.* $400-500

GTO Sport Fun, late 1960s, clay wheels, 24 inches long. *Courtesy Ed Economy.* $100-200

Makaha Molokai, 19" long, solid oak. *Courtesy Ed Economy.* $200-300

Molokai by Surf Skater. *Courtesy Ed Economy.* $200-400

Rolla-Board by Royal Surfer, made in Great Britain, 29 inches long. *Courtesy Ed Economy.* $400-500

LEFT to RIGHT:
Sidewalk Surfboard by Nash, Kiss Me model, 22 inches. *Courtesy Ed Economy.* $200-250

Made from solid Koa wood with clay wheels, this 34-inch Duke is in mint condition and can not be replaced. *Courtesy Ed Economy.* $5000-6000

Sidewalk Surfboard by Champion, steel wheels, 23 inches long. *Courtesy Ed Economy.* $600-700

Flying Ace Red Surfer, solid core, by Mohen in Lancaster, Pennsylvania. Steel wheels, 24 inches long. *Courtesy Ed Economy.* $200-300

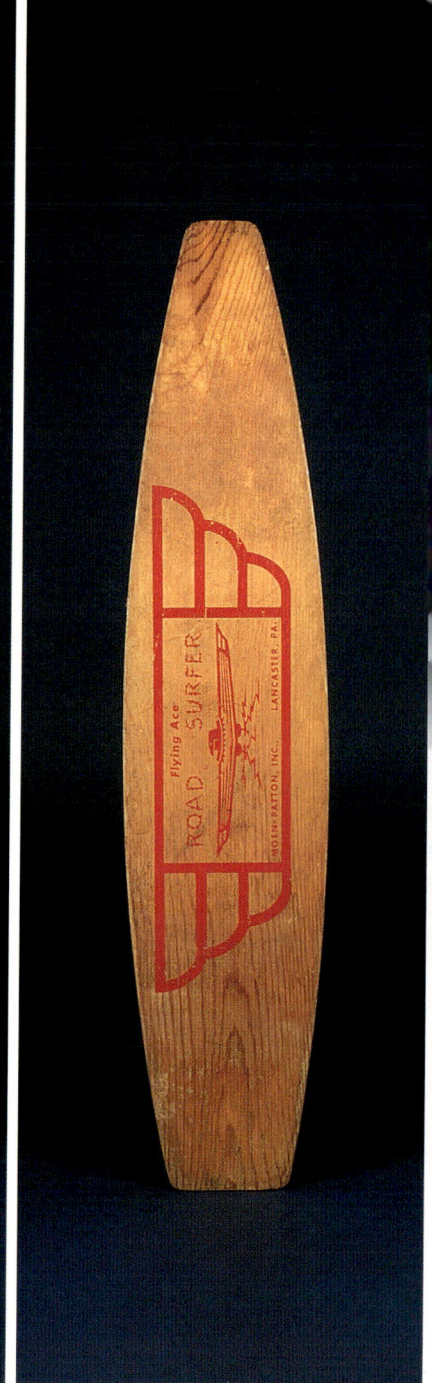

LEFT to RIGHT:

Makaha laminated hard wood, clay wheels, 29 inches long. *Courtesy Ed Economy.* $300-400

Roll and Surf by Health Way, oak and mahogany, clay wheels, 28 inches long. *Courtesy Ed Economy.* $200-300

Silver Arrow by Sport Fun, one of the earliest. 9-ply, clay wheels, 29 inches long. *Courtesy Ed Economy.* $100-200

Bat-board by Leisure Line, 9-ply, clay wheels, 26 inches long. *Courtesy Ed Economy.* $300-500

RIGHT to LEFT:
Hawaiian Surf # 50,
with Union hardware
and clay wheels.
Courtesy Ed Economy.
$300-400

Wipeout from Sears,
with wood and
fiberglass construction,
clay wheels, 27 inches
long. *Courtesy Ed
Economy.* $300-500

Rolla-Board Royal
Surfer from Great
Britain, solid wood
core, with an early
rubber wheel, 29
inches long. *Courtesy
Ed Economy.* $300-500

Boss Man, mahogany
ply, from Sport Fun.
Chicago trucks and
wheels, 24 inches long.
Courtesy Ed Economy.
$100-200

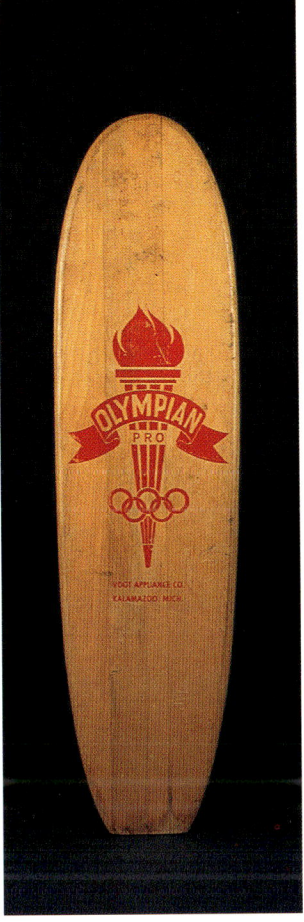
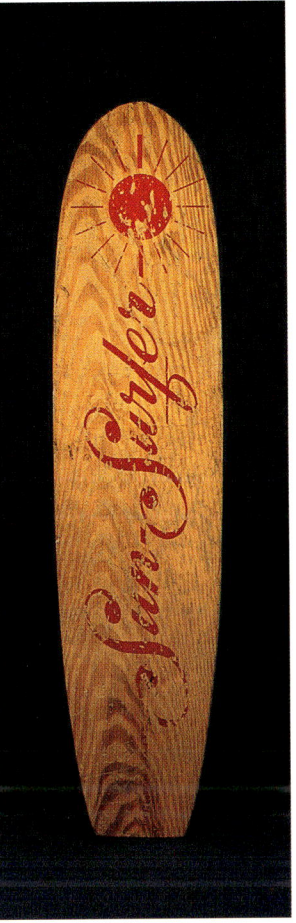
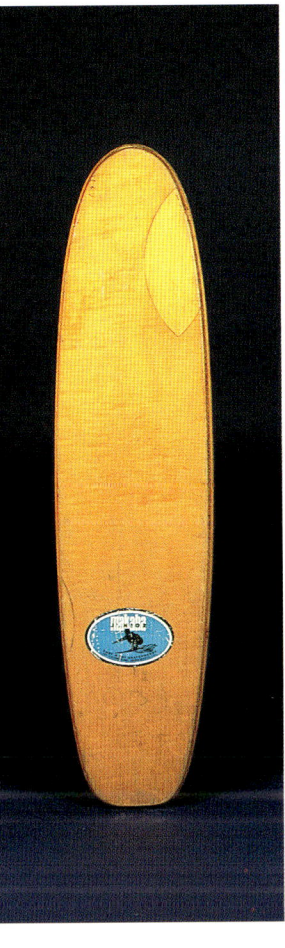

LEFT to RIGHT:

Sidewalk Surfboard by Nash, unique grip tape, clay wheels, 22 inches long. *Courtesy Ed Economy.* $150-200

Olympian Pro, made by Bogt Appliance Company, Kalamazoo, Michigan. Clay wheels, 22 inches long. *Courtesy Ed Economy.* $300-400

Sun Surfer, Chicago wheels and trucks, 22 inches long. *Courtesy Ed Economy.* $200-300

Makaha Jr., 6-ply, steel wheels, 19 inches. *Courtesy Ed Economy.* $200-300

Duke, laminated hardwood, clay wheels, 26 inches long, by Nash. *Courtesy Ed Economy.* $1200-1500

Mercury Skateboard, steel wheels, 19 inches long, very rare. *Courtesy Ed Economy.* $300-400

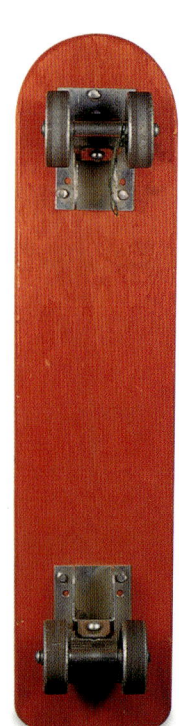

Skate-n-Glide, steel wheels, 19 inches long. *Courtesy Ed Economy.* $200-300

Surfer, steel wheels, 22 inches long. *Courtesy Ed Economy.* $200-300

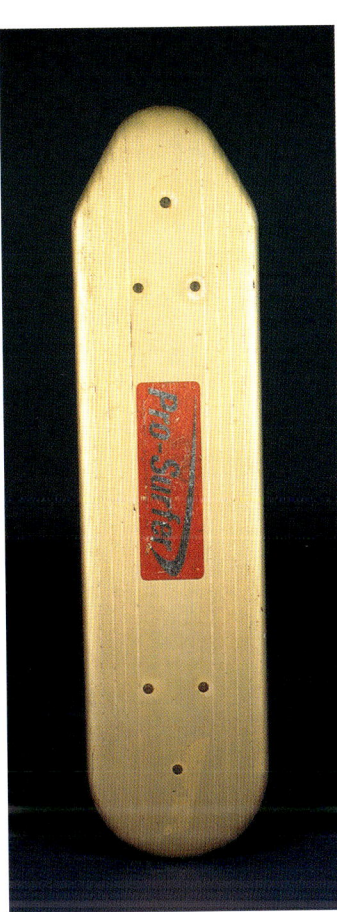

LEFT: Pro Surfer, made from gold-aluminum by New Jersey Aluminum Company in North Brunswick, New Jersey. Clay wheels, 23 inches long. *Courtesy Ed Economy.* $200-300

RIGHT: Pro Surfer, aluminum construction, silver model, 23 inches long. *Courtesy Ed Economy.* $200-300

The Woody by Sears, steel wheels, 5-ply, 23 inches long. This one is mint. *Courtesy Ed Economy.* $500-600

Nash Sidewalk Surfboard by Champion, 22 inches long. *Courtesy Ed Economy.* $200-300

Red Duke, 22 inches long, steel wheels, mint condition, by Nash. *Courtesy Ed Economy.* $800-1000

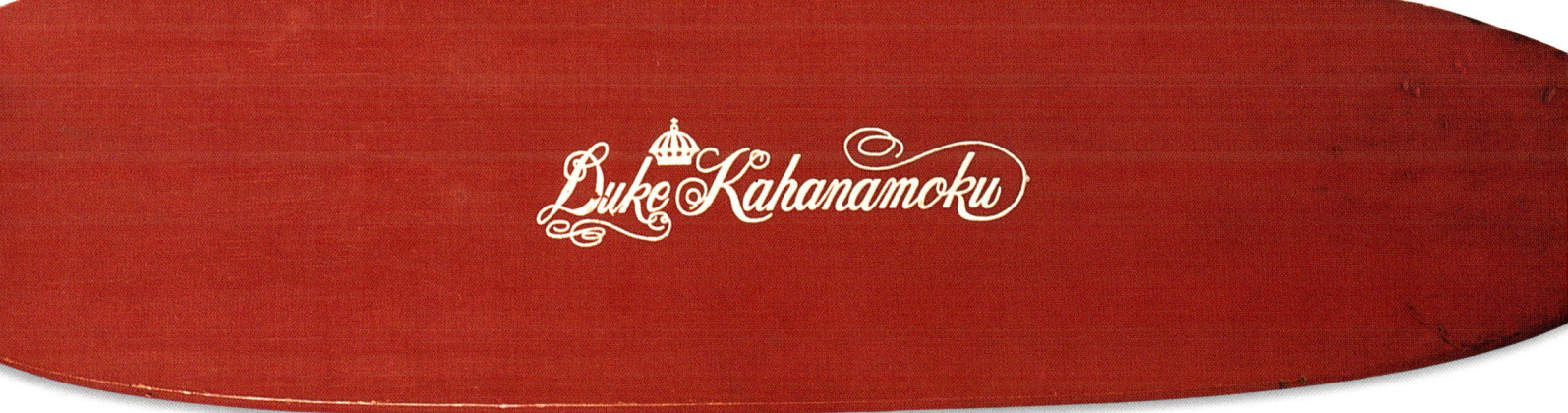

OPPOSITE PAGE; LEFT to RIGHT:

Zippees Sidewalk Surfboard, made in Chicago. Steel wheels, 23 inches long. *Courtesy Ed Economy.* $200-300

Hobie Super Surfer, early Dana Point Model, 30 inches long, clay wheels. *Courtesy Ed Economy.* $1000-1500, this board is mint.

Sidewalk Surfboard by Nash. Solid wood core, clay wheels, rare graphics, 23 inches long. *Courtesy Ed Economy.* $500-600

Ultimate, by Sport Fun. 9-ply, early green urethane wheel, 28 inches long. *Courtesy Ed Economy.* $200-300

LEFT to RIGHT: Roller Derby #20 with Roller Derby wheels, 22 inches long. *Courtesy Ed Economy.* $100-200

Surfer with clay wheels, 22 inches long. *Courtesy Ed Economy.* $200-300

Starburst by Nash. Beveled rail, clay wheels, 24 inches long. *Courtesy Ed Economy.* $200-300

Zippees' Sidewalk Surfboard. Steel wheels, 27 inches long. $200-300

LEFT: Sears Hot Dog, clay wheels, 29 inches long. *Courtesy Ed Economy.* $200-300

RIGHT: Zippees Sidewalk Surfboard All Pro, steel wheels, 26 inches long. *Courtesy Ed Economy.* $200-300

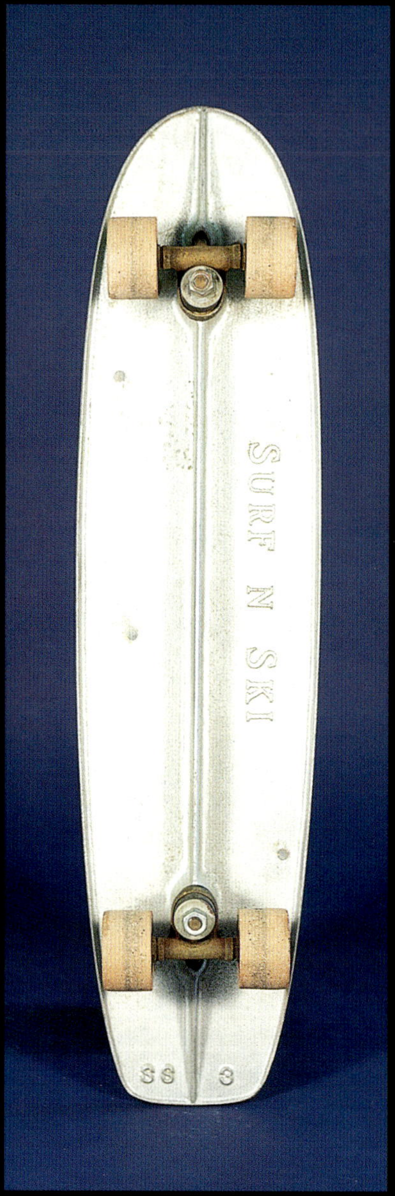

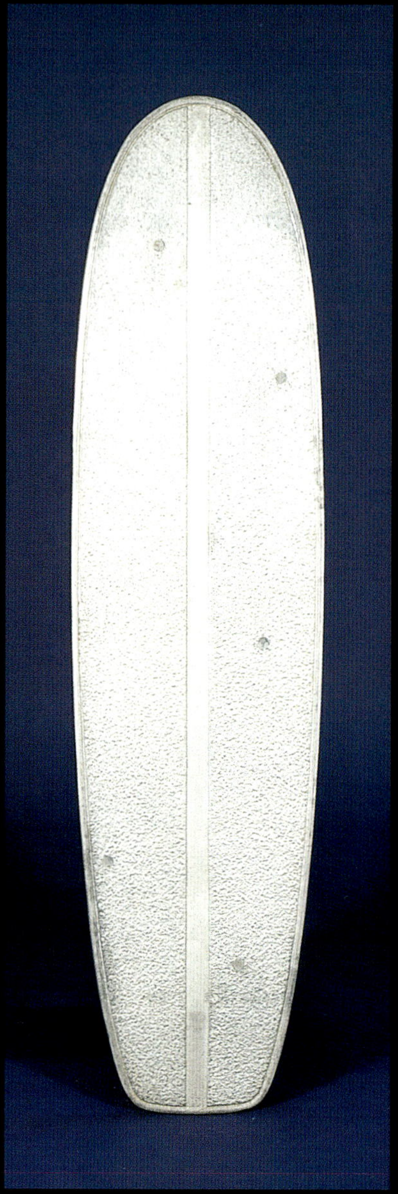

Surf and Ski. A rare aluminum molded factory press, clay Chicago wheels, 24 inches long. Made in El Monte, California. Originally sold for $17.00, now worth $500-600. *Courtesy Ed Economy.*

54

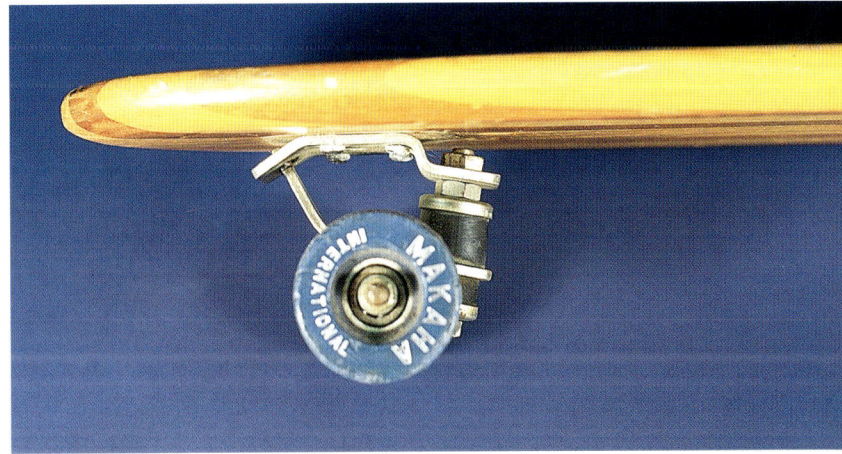

LEFT to RIGHT:
Roller Derby with early rubber wheels, 20 inches long. *Courtesy Ed Economy.* $100-200

Makaha Malibu, one of only two known to exist. Steel wheels, 19 inches long. *Courtesy Ed Economy.* $500-800

Surf Bird by Nash, steel wheels, 21 inches long. *Courtesy Ed Economy.* $100-200

Hawaiian Surf by Union, made in Philadelphia. Steel wheels. *Courtesy Ed Economy.* $200-300

LEFT to RIGHT:
Makaha Surf Skate, Chicago clay wheels, Pill Edwards Model. Made of oak, 21 inches long. *Courtesy Ed Economy.* $800-1000

Roller Surfer #100, made by Headland, steel wheels, 19 inches long. *Courtesy Ed Economy.* $200-300

Nash Waimea, clay Chicago trucks and wheels, made from solid oak, 21 inches long. *Courtesy Ed Economy.* $300-500

Neakahanee by Laudeback, Portland, Oregon. Chicago trucks and wheels, 27 inches long. *Courtesy Ed Economy.* $400-500

Surf and Skate, steel wheels, 19 inches long. *Courtesy Ed Economy.* $200-300

At Wind 'n Sea in the mid-1960s, kids were riding through drain pipes. All kinds of surfaces were being tested, but slalom and freestyle were the words of the day. Mike Hynson, a legendary surfer, had three models of skateboards, a 24-inch slalom which sold for $11.95, a 26-inch standard which sold for $14.95, a 28-inch Hynson which sold for $13.95.

Annette Funicello album with all the latest surf music, 1965. *Courtesy Ed Economy.* $100-150

Jan and Dean go sidewalk surfing with *I Gotta Drive*, 1965. *Courtesy Ed Economy.* $50-100

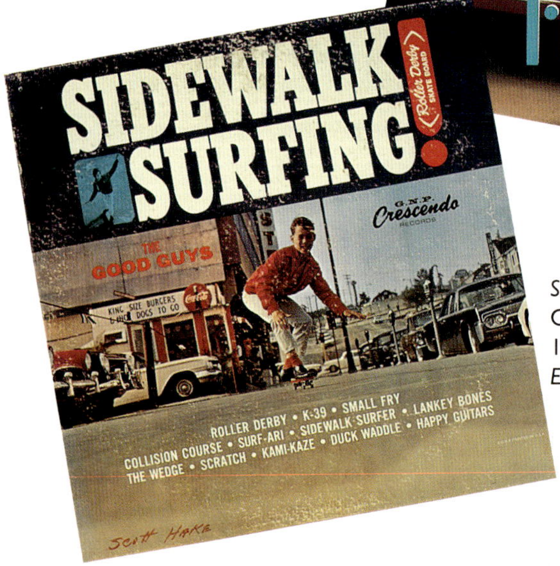

Sidewalk Surfing by Crescendo Records, 1965. *Courtesy Ed Economy.* $50-100

Cover of *Life* magazine, May 14, 1965. Photo by Bill Epperidge. *Courtesy Ed Economy.* $25-60

The Challengers Go Sidewalk Surfing by Triumph Records, 1965. *Courtesy Ed Economy.* $50-100

With this aerial view Stoner provided, Tommy Ryan's style radiates. *Courtesy Classic Stoner Photos.*

The 1965 International Championships were in La Palma Stadium, Anaheim, California, on May 22 and 23—the first major competition ever, which received coverage on all three of the national television networks, CBS, NBC, and ABC. A $500 scholarship was awarded to the winners.

Ski Skate, a Culver City, California based company sold 500,000 boards at the price of $3.00 each. Duke Kahanamoku (1890-1968), the legendary Hawaiian surfer and Olympic champion, lent his name to a skateboard line. To date, Duke skateboards command the highest values.

This photo is for all who doubt that the sport is a part of American history: 1965 Nationals in Anaheim. *Courtesy Classic Stoner Photos.*

Skaterdater soundtrack by Mira Records, 1966. *Courtesy Ed Economy.* $50-100

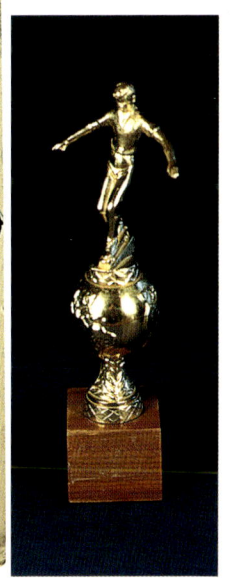

John Freiz, Overall Grand Champion, with his $500.00 *Skateboarder Magazine* Scholarship. *Courtesy Classic Stoner Photos.*

1965 Vida Pakt Trophy. *Courtesy Ed & Randy Economy.*

Skateboarding continued to flourish in 1965. International skateboard champion John Freeze, Dave and Stevie, the Hilton Brothers, Skip Feye, and Bruce Logan were creating exciting and innovative moves. Music from Jan and Dean's *Sidewalk Surfing* fanned the flames. Skateboarding spread to Canada, Japan, Europe, Australia, New Zealand and South Africa. From the Taj Mahal to the Golden Gate Bridge, skateboard popularity exploded. *The Quarterly Skateboarder* magazine got it start in 1965. Warren Bosler was the editor.

Courtesy Jim Phillips.

Danny Bearer with toes over. He was called the White Knight of 1965. *Courtesy Classic Stoner Photos.*

Joey Cabell and Torger Johnson demonstrating early beer can slalom. *Courtesy Classic Stoner Photos.*

Danny Hilton and his classic curb jump at night, 1965. *Courtesy Classic Stoner Photos.*

Roy Diedrichsen's backyard pool in Menlo Park was one of the first vert surfaces to be tested. It was featured in an article in first issue of *The Quarterly Skateboarder* in 1965. There was another early pool used for skateboarding, called "Foxtail Park," located in Santa Monica, California.

Steve Hilton pulls some early vert in a pool at Foxtail Park. *Courtesy Classic Stoner Photos.*

Just outside of Santa Monica, a pool in Fox Tail Park, an unknown skater with clay wheels. With an ominous-looking moat at the bottom, he verts his way through what could possibly be the first pool ever ridden. March 1965. *Courtesy Classic Stoner Photos.*

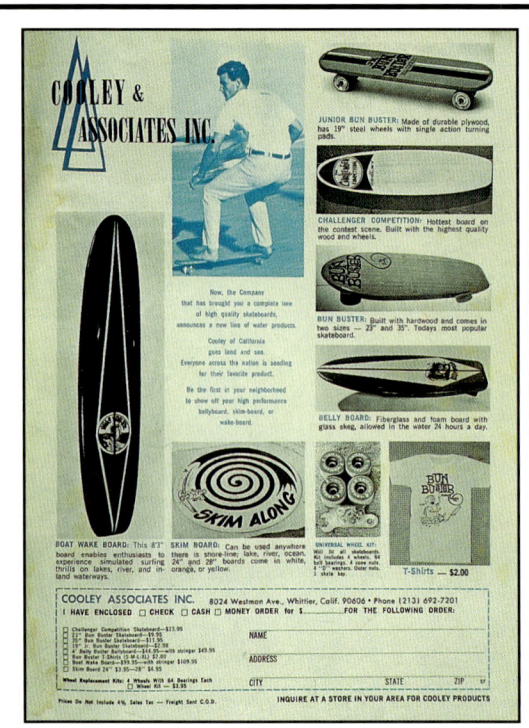

Classic early skate ads from *Surfing Illustrated*. George Cooley created Bun Buster. *Courtesy Roger Graves*.

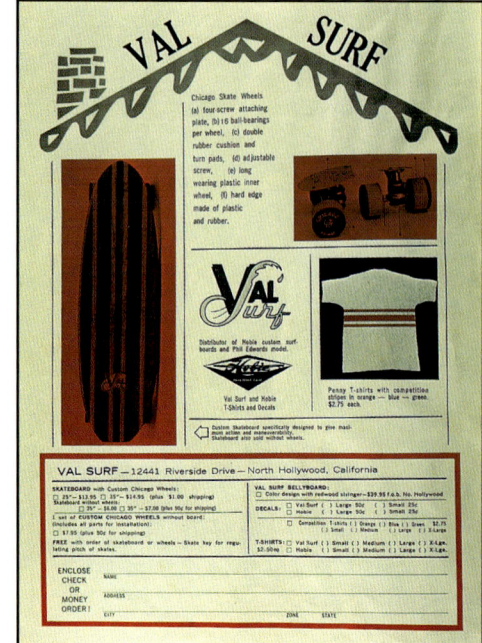

Classic early skate ads from *Surfing Illustrated* for Val Surf. Note the cool t-shirts and the Hobie Decks with the red capped wheels. *Courtesy Roger Graves*.

Early coupon from one of the first issues of *Skateboarder* Magazine. *Courtesy Tom Craig*.

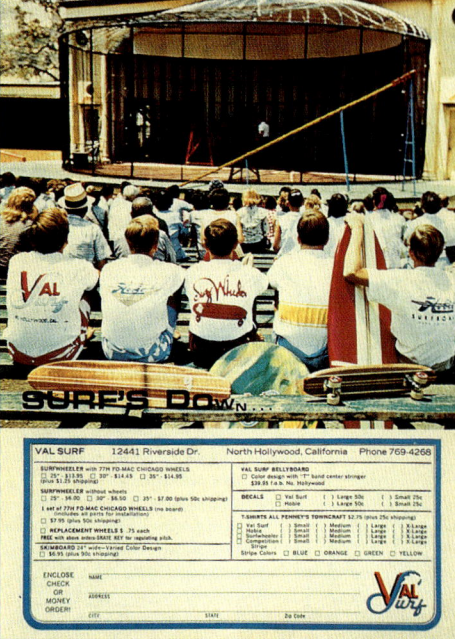

Covers of the earliest *Skate Board* magazines. $250 each, $600-800 for the set.

In 1964 *Quarterly Skateboard* magazine arrived, emphasizing Tony Ryan, Mickey Maga, Dave and Steve Hilton, Torger Johnson, Danny Schaeffer, and Pat McGee, transforming them into media stars. The magazine ended publication in Fall of 1965. These covers appeared in *Skateboarder*, 1980. *Courtesy Ed Economy.*

In 1966 the sport of skateboarding crashed for the first time. Bad injuries and even fatalities forced companies to reconsider wheel design, but clay remained the cheapest way to make a wheel. While the first laws to ban skateboarding were enacted in the mid-1960s, because of reports of injuries, cities and law enforcement increased the pressure against skateboarding, turning the boom to a bust...for a while at least.

• 1967: *Gilligan's Island* was canceled.
• Late 1960s: The Vietnam conflict loomed over the country.
• Man landed on the Moon in 1969.

In the midst of the times some monumental developments in the skateboard took place. Larry Stevenson's first recollection of skateboards was when Larry and his brother were in an orphanage in the late 1930s. A man named Leo Careo came out every other weekend to bring toys to the kids. One weekend he brought orange crate scooters, and a week or so later the orange crates got knocked off. Larry and his brother skated on them and subsequently became fathers to skateboarding. A lifeguard and publisher of the *Surf Guide*, he acquired the patent for his Kicktail in 1969. It was a design to angle one or both ends of the board to give the rider more leverage and vastly expanding the capabilities of the board. With this he breathed new life into skateboarding. Whether it was used for a stopping mechanism, or for turning, or both, this was an instrumental development in the infancies of bending boards. If you track kicktails and concaves, this is where they started.

Mike Purpus demonstrating Larry's kick tail. *Courtesy Leroy Grannis.*

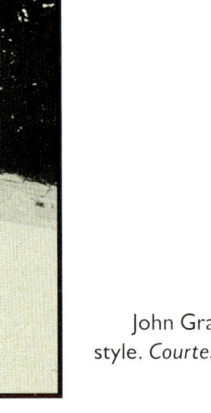

John Grannis in barefoot style. *Courtesy Leroy Grannis.*

Larry Stevenson's Surf Guide, 1965. *Courtesy Roger Graves.*

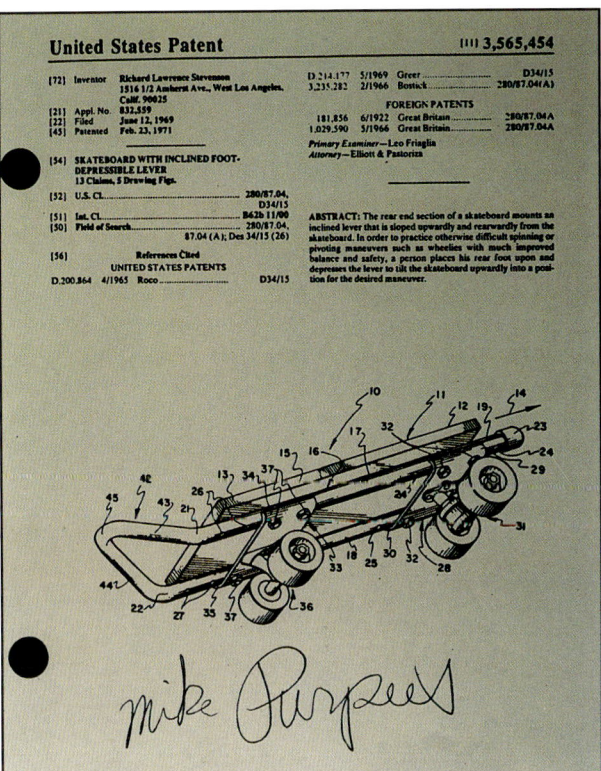

Larry Stevenson patent, signed by Mike Purpus. *Courtesy Dale Smith*

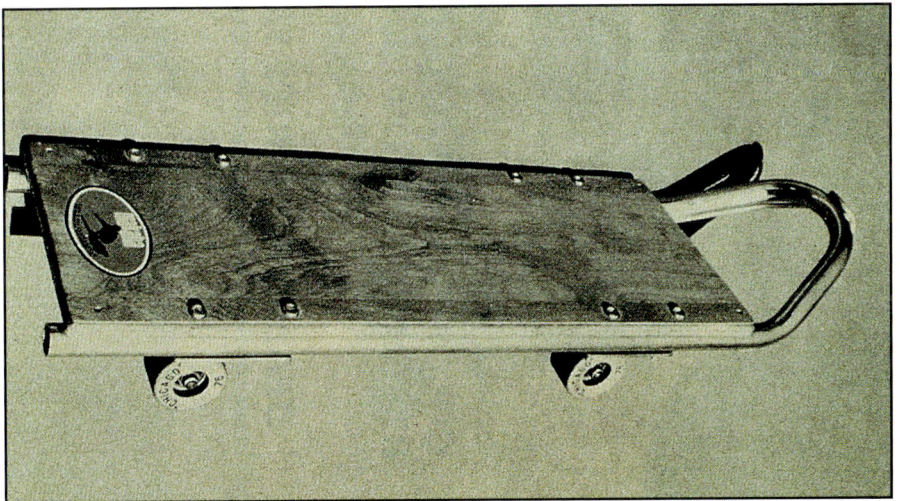

Larry Stevenson is accredited for the first kick tail. Whether it was for stopping or turning, the foot lever was a milestone. *Courtesy Leroy Grannis.*

Chapter 3

The 1970s

1971: Hot Pants were in.

The sport was poised for new advancements in wheel and truck design. The urethane barrier was about to be broken. Urethane had been around since the 1930s, and in fact was already being used on some skateboards, but was not mainstream yet. In 1970 Frank Nasworthy traveled to Virginia to meet with Vernon Heightfield, who was working on wheels for Roller Sports, a chain of roller rinks. Trying the new wheels on a skateboard Frank and his friends were amazed at the quality of the ride. Before long Frank was marketing a skateboarding version of these wheels, becoming the creator of the Cadillac Urethane Skateboard Wheel.

Two classic Cadillac Wheels ads from the *Skateboard Handbook*. Courtesy James O'Mahoney.

A set of Cadillac Stoker wheels, Sure-Grip trucks, and drop bearings.

This milestone in the skateboard's history, when added to the publicity attracted by the skate teams, gave the skateboard national exposure and broke it out of its doldrums.

This new development and advancements in truck designs helped to make the 1970s what many consider to be the heyday of skateboarding. Though abandoned swimming pools had been a popular spot for skateboarding since the early years, the new urethane wheels meant that vert could now be skated. The urethane wheel had better traction and allowed for a more forgiving ride. Thanks to urethane, we were delivered out of the claywheel stone age.

This is a part of a sequence shot from Steve Monahan getting cooled off. *Courtesy James O' Mahoney.*

Hitting high. *Courtesy Leroy Grannis.*

Jim Higham getting some early '70s vert. *Courtesy James O' Mahoney.*

Kicktails, wide trucks, and precision bearings were also milestones of this era.

Sunburst on Pure Juiced. *Courtesy James O' Mahoney.*

An early move called "Crack the Jack". *Courtesy James O' Mahoney.*

Bob Jarvis stalling with style.
Courtesy James O' Mahoney.

Tina Trefethen showing an elegant one-footed nose wheelie. *Courtesy James O'Mahoney.*

Monahan at Rocket Ship Park. *Courtesy James O'Mahoney.*

Gymnastics played a large part in women's freestyle in the '70s. Skater Tina Trefethen. *Courtesy James O'Mahoney.*

Jeff O' Mahoney, Jim's son, showing off some of his dad's moves: the two-board bomb and the two-board nose wheelie. *Courtesy James O'Mahoney.*

69

By 1973, skateboarding felt a second wave of popularity due to the urethane breakthrough. The favorite terrain became street spillways and reservoirs. Ron Bennett created his first truck with skateboarding in mind. Tracker Trucks followed in 1974, created by Dave Dominy.

Through the funnel in L.A. *Courtesy James O' Mahoney*

The Velodrome being tested by early longboarders. *Courtesy James O' Mahoney.*

Sims in grand style, cruising the dam in Encino, California. *Courtesy James O' Mahoney*

Jim Higham and O'Mahoney go for it down extremely dangerous L.A. County spillway, appropriately named the "Widow Maker." *Courtesy James O' Mahoney.*

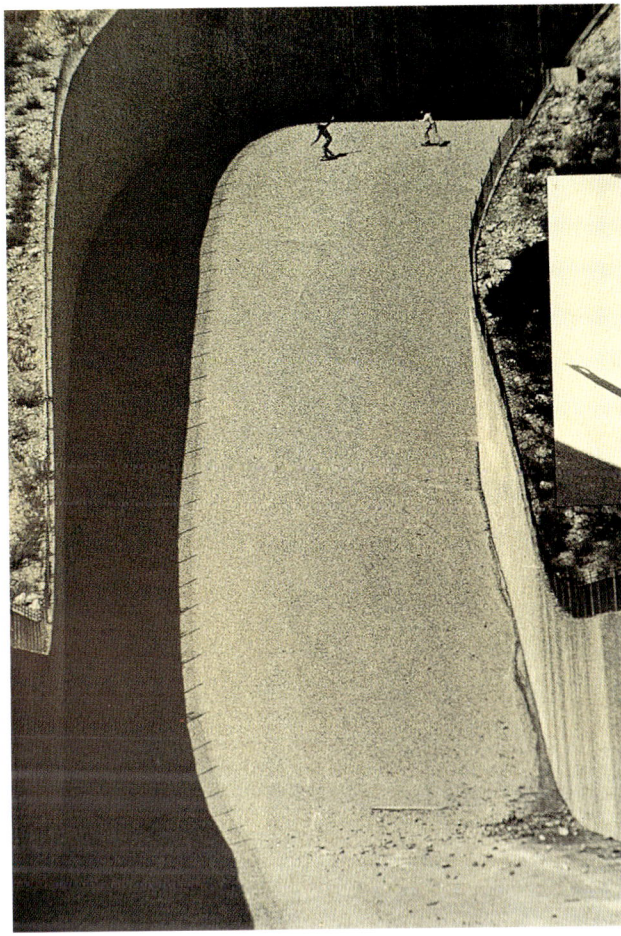

Jay Adams at the Olympic Velodrome. *Courtesy James O' Mahoney.*

Kevin Anderson. *Courtesy Leroy Grannis.*

Concrete waves from Hawaii to Hollywood. The drought was here and spillways and reservoirs were high and dry. *Courtesy James O' Mahoney.*

Bob Jarvis, spinning grace. *Courtesy James O'Mahoney.*

Diamond Bowl. *Courtesy James O'Mahoney.*

Tony Alva in a classic walk to the nose, Hawaii. *Courtesy Steve Wilkings.*

By 1974 the skate industry was once again in boom times. It was a legitimate sport, with sponsors, competition, media magazines, and lots of companies competing for a place in the skate market. Skateboard trucks and wheels have changed dramatically. The new trucks allowed the skateboard to fly higher, turn tighter, and go faster. This influenced style, tricks, and the evolution of the skateboard. From carve to vert, this era saw an incredible number of changes. Skaters dwell in the weightlessness of riding pools.

Laura Thornhill, hair in motion, pulling a 360. *Courtesy James O' Mahoney.*

Cal Jam 2, Ty Page in early free former regalia. *Courtesy James O' Mahoney.*

Ty Page takes first place at Santa Barbara. *Courtesy James O' Mahoney.*

Peggy Oki accepts trophy for first place in women's slalom. *Courtesy James O' Mahoney.*

Bruce Logan pulling a fifteen-second nose wheelie at the First National Bahne Cadillac Skateboard Championships. *Courtesy Leroy Grannis.*

Russ stops the show with his routine at the First National Bahne Cadillac Championships. *Courtesy Leroy Grannis.*

74

FREE FORMER TEAM DEMO, CALIFORNIA JAM II, ONTARIO MOTOR SPEEDWAY MARCH 18, 1978

PHOTO BY JIM O. MAHONEY

In 1978, Brian Beardsley was the High Jump World Champ. *Courtesy James O' Mahoney.*

Ty Page with a fantastic headstand *Courtesy Leroy Grannis.*

Downhill finish at the Bahne-Cadillac Skateboard Championships.

The view from the top of a slalom course. *Courtesy Leroy Grannis.*

75

Ty Page nose wheelies the length of the course at the Cal State University, Northridge Skateboard Jam. *Courtesy James O' Mahoney.*

Debbie Elldridge competes at the Skateboard Jam. *Courtesy James O' Mahoney*

T. Curren, a young crowd pleaser. *Courtesy James O' Mahoney.*

Skitch Hitchcock doing a handstand. *Courtesy Leroy Grannis.*

Downhill at Catalina. *Courtesy Rich Novak and NHS.*

Tom Sims kick turns his longboard into the history books. *Courtesy James O' Mahoney.*

LEFT: Fred Flavell spread out. *Courtesy James O' Mahoney.*

RIGHT: Matt Smith goes into his routine in front of the USSA judges. *Courtesy James O' Mahoney.*

Cal Jam 2. Jim gives us a great overview of 400,000 people in Riverside County. *Courtesy James O'Mahoney.*

Wentzel Ruml bank grinds. *Courtesy James O' Mahoney.*

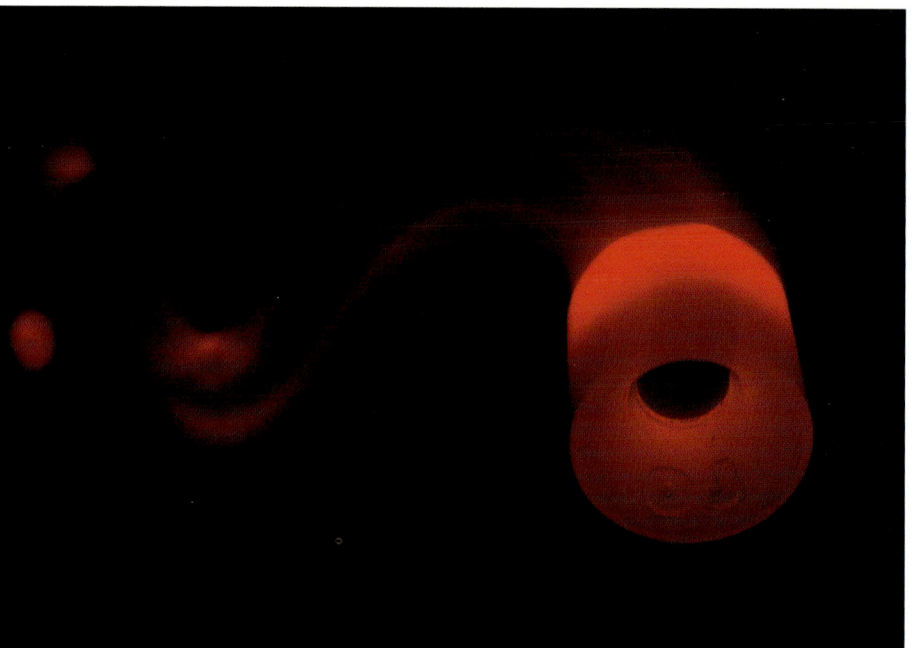

Mark Thumper pulls off a good hand stand at Santa Barbara City Championships. *Courtesy James O' Mahoney*

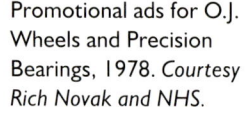

Promotional ads for O.J. Wheels and Precision Bearings, 1978. *Courtesy Rich Novak and NHS.*

Classic park vert. *Courtesy Rich Novak, NHS, and Jim Phillips.*

In 1975 NHS, Santa Cruz Skate Company came on the scene, with the Road Rider wheel and the precision bearing, and, later, the Park Rider. These developments ended the loose ball bearing era. In Southern California Jim O'Mahoney did much to promote the sport and formed the US Skateboard Association. He also produced three skateboard publications, one called *Skateboard*.

Early Road Rider ad. *Courtesy Rich Novak and NHS.*

Between the Independent Truck, Park Rider, Precision Bearing, and Road Rider Wheels, NHS has made quite a contribution. *Courtesy Rich Novak and NHS.*

1975 promotional ads, OJ and Road Rider. *Courtesy Todd Huber, Rich Novak, and NHS.*

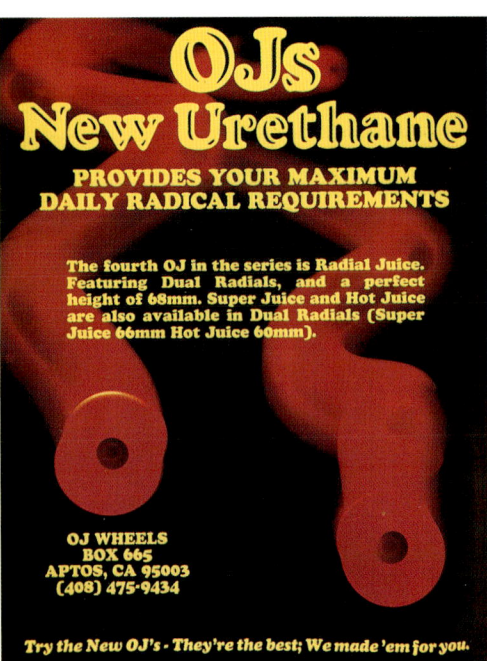

OJ Urethane ad. *Courtesy James O' Mahoney, Rich Novak, and NHS.*

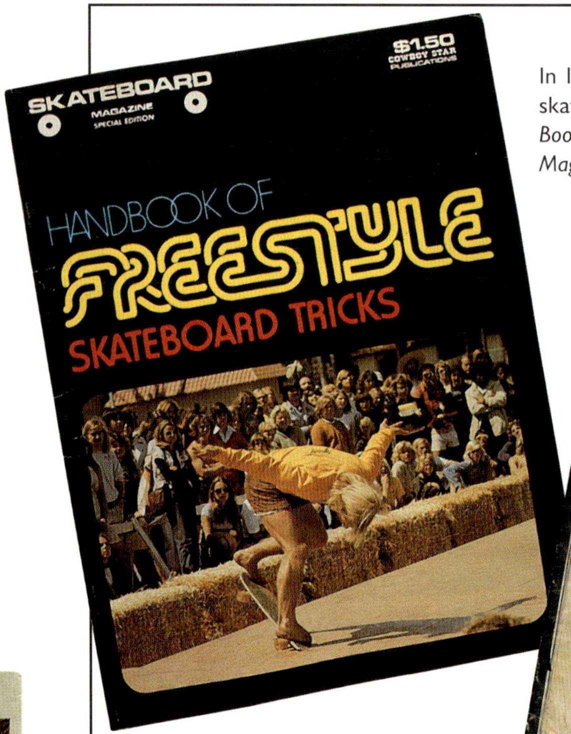

OJs New Urethane

PROVIDES YOUR MAXIMUM DAILY RADICAL REQUIREMENTS

The fourth OJ in the series is Radial Juice. Featuring Dual Radials, and a perfect height of 68mm. Super Juice and Hot Juice are also available in Dual Radials (Super Juice 66mm Hot Juice 60mm).

OJ WHEELS
BOX 665
APTOS, CA 95003
(408) 475-9434

Try the New OJ's - They're the best; We made 'em for you.

In 1975, Jim O'Mahoney published three skateboard magazines: *Skateboard Handbook, Book of Freestyle Tricks,* and *Skateboard Magazine.*

Early Santa Cruz skate ad featuring John Hudson. *Courtesy Jim Phillips.*

Dogtown's Zephyr team, featuring Tony Alva, Jay Adams, and Stacy Peralta changed the face of skating. When I was a kid in the early 1970s, guys like Greg Weaver and Tony Alva blew my mind. Russ Howell, Steve Cathy, Connie Toft, Dale Smith, Mike Weed, the Logan Brothers and many others were at the forefront of the decade. Surf and skate were one, they were part of the same mechanism. Skateboard championships were also held at Del Mar.

We all remember this shot. Wallos Carve by Tony Alva. *Courtesy Steve Wilkings.*

Tony Alva's style and grace captured a generation of skate-stoked minds. Here he is in the sweetest environment on the planet, Hawaii. *Courtesy Steve Wilkings.*

Brad Logan, in classic form, nose wheelies with Tony Alva looking on. *Courtesy Steve Wilkings.*

A unique duel-axle truck produced by Bennett. *Courtesy James O'Mahoney.*

Olie the Wonder Dog in true skating form. *Courtesy James O'Mahoney.*

The Boehne's tandem skating. *Courtesy James O' Mahoney.*

In 1975 *SkateBoarder* magazine resumed publication. Equipment started to catch up with the sport. Ron Bennett made the Bennett Hijacker truck, which had technological innovations and quality demanded by freestyle boarders. Vertical riding was everywhere. Nathan Pratt was getting some early air with straps on his board. Greg Weaver was riding old water skis in an early example of long board skateboarding. Tom Sims was one of the first to build a long board skateboard, and others followed suit simultaneously. In those days skaters had "quivers," different boards for different situations.

Cover shot of *Skateboarding Magazine* featuring Greg Weaver. *Courtesy Ed Economy.* $40-100

Ed Economy with early longboard vert. *Courtesy Ed Economy. Photo: Perez*

Ed Economy with his long board quiver. *Photo Jim Goodrich.*

Tom Sims demonstrates his surfing style through riding a longboard. *Courtesy James O' Mahoney*

Dale Shull, getting some longboard vert. *Courtesy James O'Mahoney.*

Andy Pryciak, riding what seems to be over eight feet of board. *Courtesy James O'Mahoney.*

Make Room For
LONGBOARDING

Andy Pryciak rides his contribution to the longboarding movement. Photo: O'Mahoney.

Steve and Barrie Boehne's high stag lay back tandem surfing in the streets. *Courtesy James O'Mahoney.*

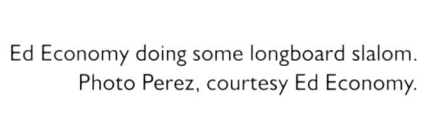

Ed Economy doing some longboard slalom.
Photo Perez, courtesy Ed Economy.

One-footed nose wheelie by Mark Boden. *Courtesy James O'Mahoney.*

Photo by Jim O'Mahoney

The first skate parks opened in the summer of 1976. John O'Malley and Jack Graham opened the Carlsbad Skate park in California. An outdoor skate park opened in Jacksonville, Florida called Skate City, and Surfers World opened in Anaheim, California. Jack Smith recalls a city park in Visalia, California called Minigroove back in 1964. Smith was the pioneer of the sand board, a kind of snowboarding on sand dunes. He also was the first to skate from coast to coast, starting in Lebanon, Oregon, through the Rockies, through the Appalachians, and ending in Williamsburg, Virginia 32 days later. He did this skate with two other skaters in a relay fashion for the Multiple Sclerosis charity in 1976. He repeated the journey in 1984.

Images from Aala park in Hawaii. *Courtesy Steve Wilkings.*

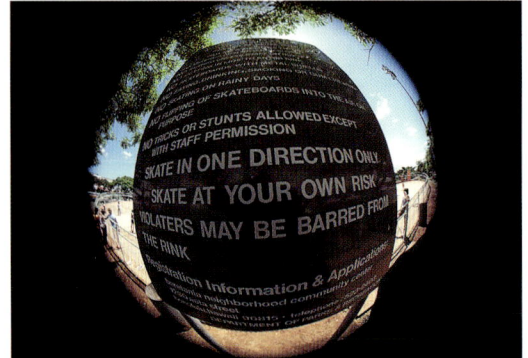

A classic pool party in paradise with Chris Owens, Vince Klyn, and Jasper as the hosts. *Courtesy Steve Wilkings.*

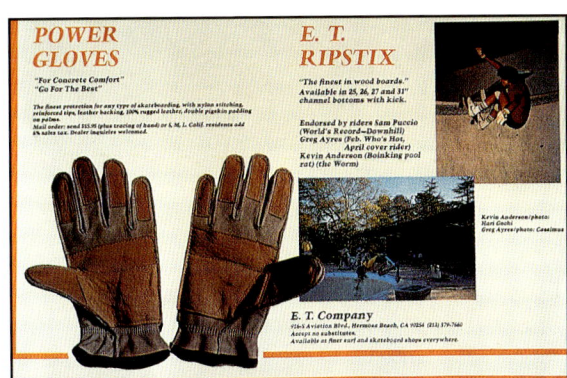

ET Surfboard ad.
Courtesy ET Surf-
boards.

Promotional ad for
ET Fiberflex. *Courtesy*
ET Surfboards.

Warning posted at
the Wallos, Hawaii.
Courtesy Steve
Wilkings.

Roy Russell with early park grind.
Courtesy Steve Wilkings.

Local kids skating in Hawaii. *Courtesy Steve Wilkings.*

Jeff O'Mahoney on a 1970s Rocket Skate. Celebrating the country's Bicentennial. *Courtesy James O' Mahoney.*

Jay Adams in classic early '70s form at Uluwatu, Hawaii. *Courtesy Steve Wilkings.*

Gary Owens at Aala Park in Hawaii. *Courtesy Steve Wilkings.*

Images to behold, Gerry Lopez skating the Wallos—historic carves by the pipemaster. *Courtesy Steve Wilkings.*

The whole connection between surf and skate. Larry Bertleman shown here going for the drop in classic style. Note the Duke Shorts. *Courtesy Steve Wilkings.*

Larry Bertleman at Uluwatu, Hawaii. *Courtesy Steve Wilkings.*

A rare shot of Torger in Hawaii, July 1975. *Courtesy Steve Wilkings.*

Jackie Dunn and Roy Russell going for some early concrete lip smacks in Hawaii. *Courtesy Steve Wilkings.*

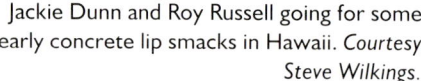

Other early pipe action. South Face Skate Park in Torrance, California. *Courtesy Jim O'Mahoney.*

The 1976 Signal Hill World Record Runs saw Sam Puccio hit 54 miles per hour on a skateboard and won the race. Michael Williams produced the Gullwing Truck, and pool riding entered a new era. Danny Way was an early pioneer in the air. Cities stamped out skating reservoirs and bowls; they were restricted indefinitely.

Waldo Autry with some early vert at Mt. Baldy. Photos featured on the cover of *Skateboard*, 1975. *Courtesy Jim O'Mahoney.*

• 1977: *Star Wars* was number one at the box office.

In 1977 the downhill slalom event was still hot in the Colorado Rockies, while top skaters jousted for rank. Mike Weed, Waldo Autry, Bob Biniak and Kevin Adderson broke new ground in the concrete tubes in 1977.

Park Rider Promotion. *Courtesy Rich Novak and NHS*

Buttons—from the '70s to the '90s, he has remained at the heart and soul of skating. Shown here on a classic fiber-flex. *Courtesy Steve Wilkings.*

Among the manufacturers, Bennett and Cadillac prevailed in the late 1970s. The irony is that skateboarding moves and products were being recycled; most had been produced or performed years earlier than claimed. Snow skiing also influenced board builders. Roller Derby reached its pinnacle. Grip tape started to appear. In the early 1970s. Vans, the skate shoe company, started to grow.

Slalom and downhill were still prevalent competitions in the late 1970s. The Signal Hill World Record Runs were held in Long Beach starting in 1975. Guy Grundy set the first record at 50 mph. A record of 57 mph was set by Henry Hester and 1977 Down Hill Slalom champion Dave Dillberg—yes, a tie! Surfing still had a major connection with skate style of the day. Concrete waves were popping up and so were the kids, in parks from Florida to California.

In 1977 Upland Park opened, offering the first tubular terrain. This era is monumental in that skateboarders grew wings and started to fly.

Signal Hill speed run. Guy Grundy established a record at 50.2 mph. *Courtesy James O' Mahoney*

1977 *Wild World of Skateboarding* covers. Worth $40-50. *Courtesy Ed Economy.*

BELOW:

LEFT: John Hutson: whatever goes down must come up. *Courtesy Jim Phillips.*

RIGHT: Steve Olson. *Courtesy Jim Phillips.*

Many people were helping the sport evolve technologically in the late 1970s. Fausto Vitello, with Rick Blackheart's help, developed an independent skateboard truck. George Powell brought a hard white urethane wheel to the market, appropriately-named Bones.

The boards also began to take on a new look. Wes Humpston was an early graphic wizard. He and Jim Muir built a line of boards with intricate graphics, bearing the Dogtown label.

Board width was over nine inches, and the Ollie was now nationwide.

Bryan Buck floating the edge. *Courtesy Rich Novak and NHS.. Photo: Krisik*

Coping Grind, notice the stylish shoes. *Courtesy Rich Novak and NHS. Photo: Chris Hick*

Doyle with an early Santa Cruz model, in true '70s form. *Courtesy Jim Phillips.*

Jim O'Mahoney, a great photographer, had the foresight to document lots of early skate history. He is responsible for submitting the word "skateboard" to the dictionary. As a top skater of the 1970s he has retained much of the knowledge and memorabilia. He has a great surf museum in Santa Barbara, California, on 16 1/2 Helena St.

In 1978, commercialism and the dollar played a larger role in the sport. Plexiglass half pipes were an interest outside of the concrete disciplines.

Sequence of Santa Cruz Team Rider with some early park air and a chrome reflective bottom. *Courtesy NHS, Rich Novak.*

James O' Mahoney escapes the burning ring of fire. *Courtesy James O' Mahoney.*

The top skaters at this time were Hester, Olson, Dunlap, Alba, Valdez, Blackhart, Bob Skoldberg, Andrecht, Grisham, Gifford, Peters, Ty Miller, Parsons, Lamar Bowman, Ty Page, Russ Howell, Rick Dunn, Tom Sims, and Chris Yandall. In 1978 some of the great long boarders were Tom Sims, Ed Economy, Brad Strandlund, John Mather, and Jeff Tatum. On another front, Richie, René, and David Carrasco rode in over 2,000 skate demos as the Pepsi Pro Team riders.

Russ Howell doing a 360 nose wheelie. *Courtesy James O' Mahoney.*

Tom Sims. *Courtesy James O' Mahoney.*

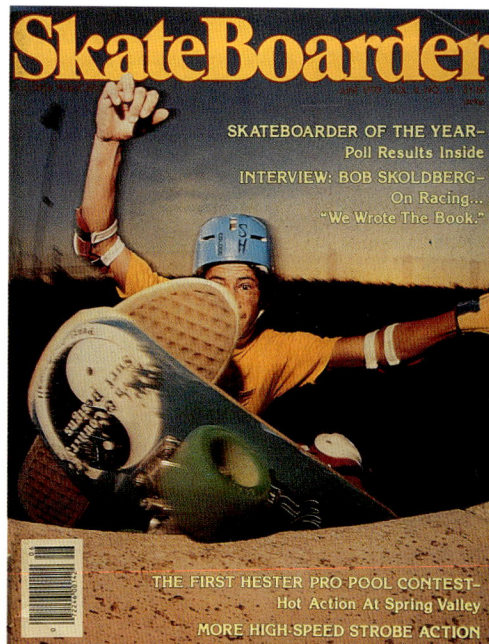

1978 cover shot of *Skateboarder Magazine. Courtesy Ed Economy.* $40-60

Andy Pryciak on an 18-foot splinter in Malibu. *Courtesy James O' Mahoney.*

In 1978 more speed records were broken at Signal Hill. Roger Williams of Hermosa Beach went 56 mph in a skate car. Tina Trefethen took first in Stand Up Downhill. It was a transitional year for everyone, which included the return of roller skating to the scene.

The search for vertical surfaces set sail for the ramps and skate parks with high-flying technical mid-air maneuvers. 1979 aerials take top consideration. Alan Gelfand was doing what was called an "Ollie pop" and no-handed Ollie aerials. Attitudes and hairstyles evolved. The Rock and Roll became a basic maneuver. The days of skate heroes seems to have died as new saplings were planted, and Powell Peralta and the Bones Brigade started the germination. Boards were going lighter, with everyone poised for the 1980s. Moves that first influenced skating were surf-oriented, but surfers were now influenced by the skate moves of the day. *Life* magazine again documented this turning point. The upstart BMX biking sport was also an influence.

Unknown skater at the dawn of the '80s. *Courtesy Rich Novak and NHS.*

From the skateboard's humble beginnings, the next three decades brought advancements in technology and technique. Trucks forward in form and function. Urethane wheels increased traction and practicality. And adding to the excitement were Kicktails, laminated boards, ollies, and the media.

The 1970s are when skating became a legitimate sport, and the boards from the 1970s are definitely collectible.

Collectors, grab them while you can. In another ten years all of these boards will triple in value. Now they're $50-200.
Courtesy James O'Mahoney

Cover from *New Times*, 1977. Courtesy Todd Huber. $20-40

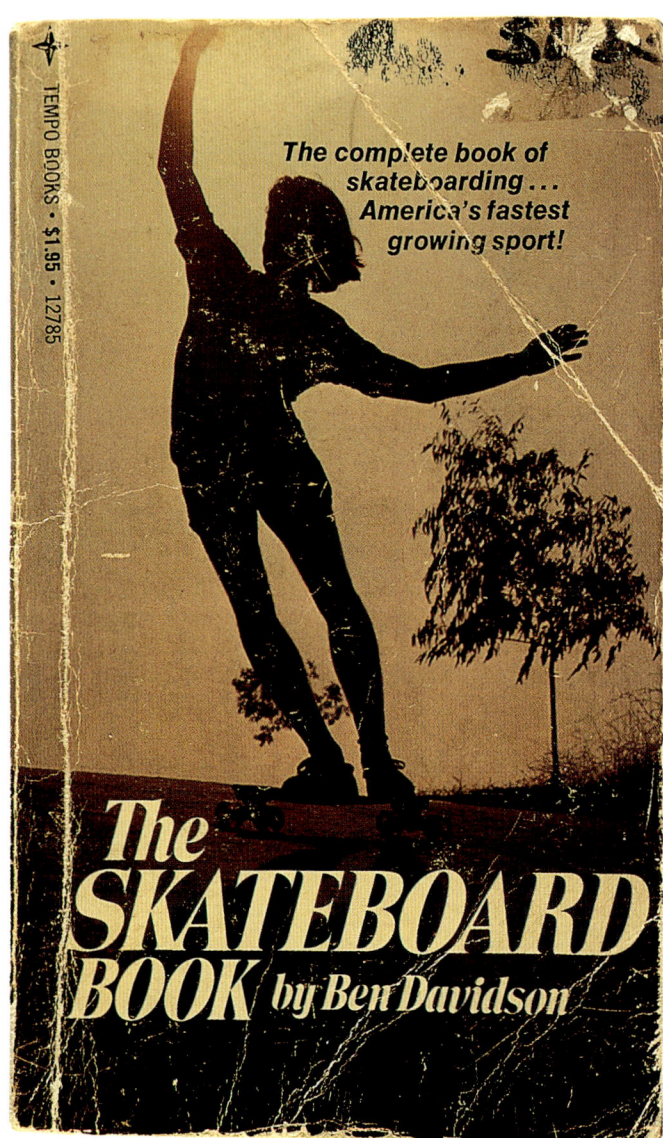

The Skateboard Book, by Ben Davidson, published by Grosset and Dunlap, is basically a how-to book. It sold for $1.95 in 1976 and is worth approximately $80 today. *Courtesy Rodney Dean.*

FOR THE BEGINNER... FOR THE EXPERT... EVERYTHING YOU NEED TO KNOW ABOUT SKATEBOARDING

The kind of skateboard that's best for you

★

Skateboarding techniques of the experts

★

How to skate well on different surfaces

★

How to fall less, and how to avoid serious injury when you do fall

★

Easy steps to exciting free-style tricks and stunts

★

The important skateboard organizations and competitions around the country

INCLUDES A SPECIAL ILLUSTRATED SECTION ON HOW TO SELECT THE BEST EQUIPMENT AND HOW TO KEEP IT IN TOP SHAPE

ILLUSTRATED WITH OVER 60 PHOTOGRAPHS AND DRAWINGS, THE SKATEBOARD BOOK PRESENTS A CLEAR, GRAPHIC GUIDE TO AMERICA'S FASTEST GROWING SPORT

The SKATEBOARD BOOK

TEMPO BOOKS

GROSSET & DUNLAP, Inc., Publishers, New York, N.Y. 10010

A FILMWAYS COMPANY

These boards, and many more, are in line for collectiblilty in the future. As each generation progresses they come into their own. All of these boards are now worth approximately $50-200. *Courtesy Todd Huber. Photo: Rhyn Noll.*

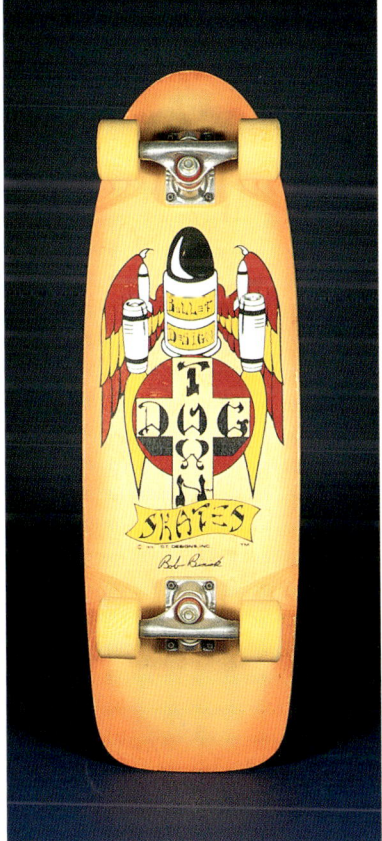

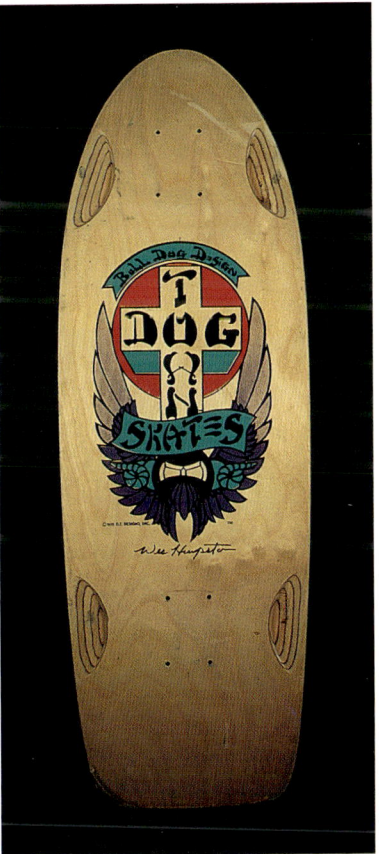

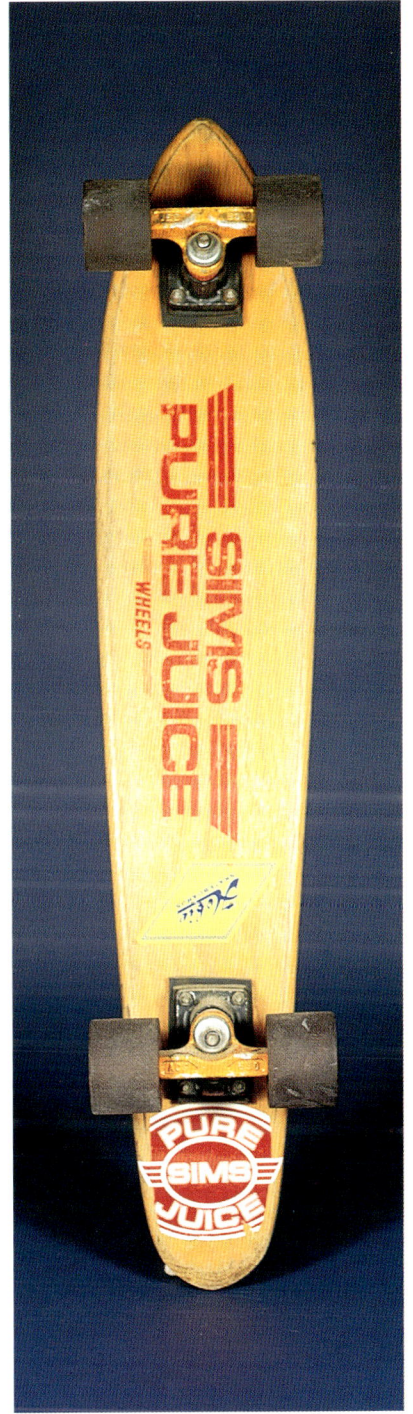

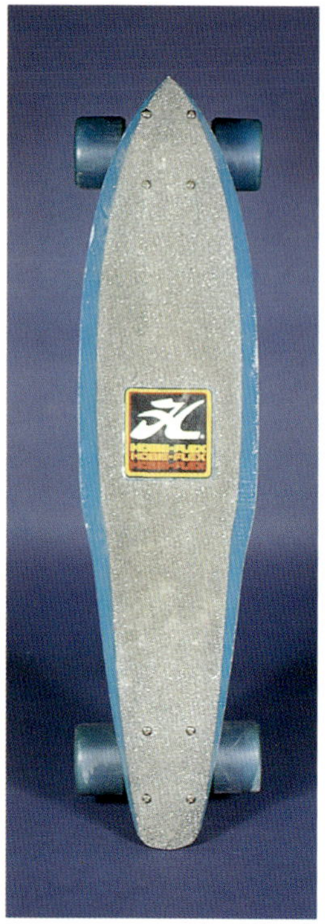

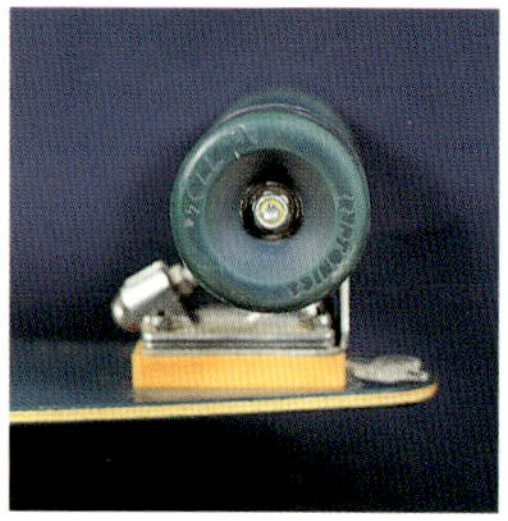

SIMS
TAPERKICK

makaha

SIMS
PURE JUICE

LandJammer

SUMMERSKI

HANG TEN
SPORT BOARD

makaha

Z-FLEX
Z-FLEX

LOGAN EARTH SKI

SIMS
LOGAN EARTH SKI
makaha

Sims Pure Juice team shirt. *Courtesy Ed Economy. Photo: Rhyn Noll*

One of the earliest Santa Cruz Skateboards. Laminated fiberglass, mint condition, worth $150. *Photo: Rhyn Noll*

Z Flex, plastic molded deck. *Courtesy Mike Gosenski. Photo: Rhyn Noll.* $50-200

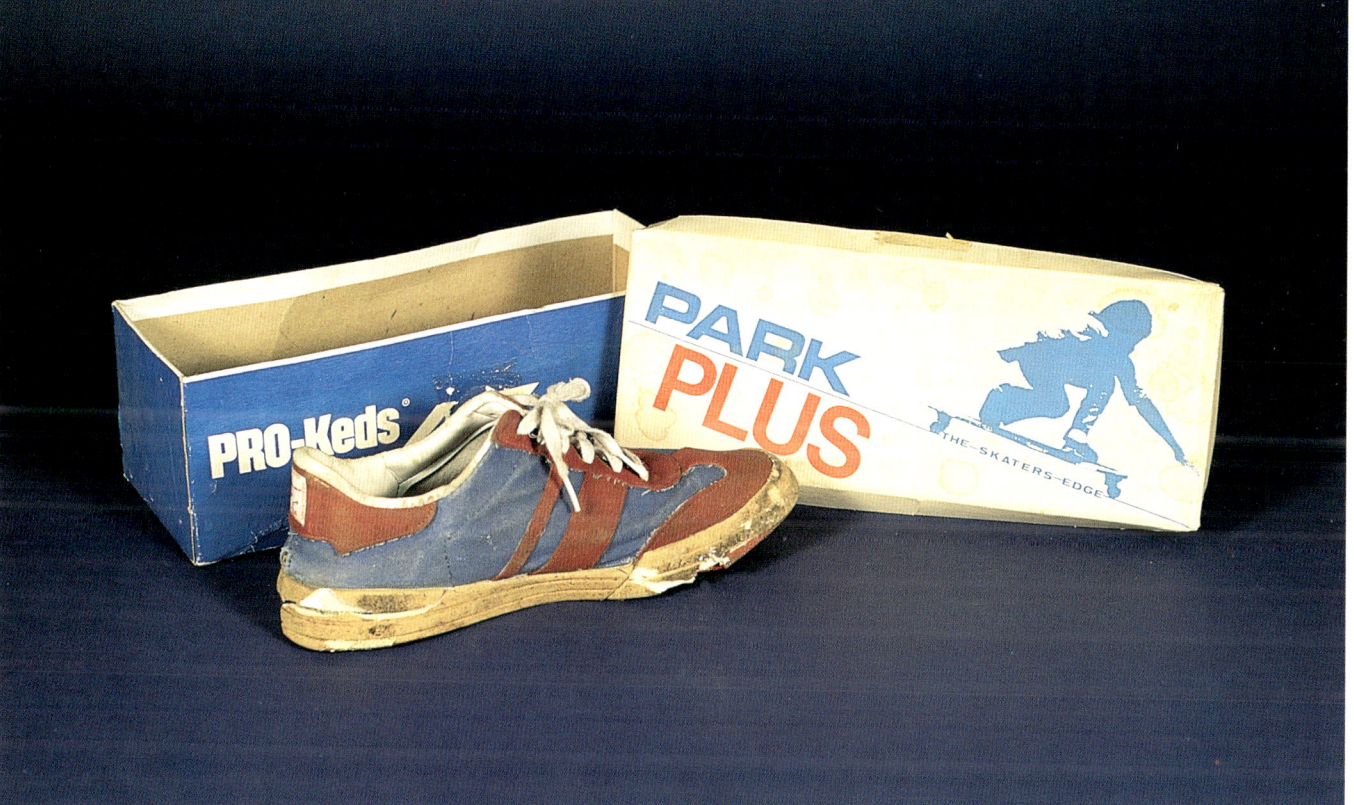

Skate memorabilia from 1975. Above: "Pro Keds" skateboarders' shoe. For most skaters, though, Vans are the original skateboard shoe. I suppose that the multi-million dollar tennis shoe of today owes a debt of gratitude to skaters and our need for a more high performance tennis shoe. Right: Tinker toy memorabilia. *Photo: Rhyn Noll.*

Solid wood Bahne. *Courtesy Mike Gosenski. Photo: Rhyn Noll.* $50-200.

Kahuna fiberglass. *Courtesy Mike Gosenski. Photo: Rhyn Noll.* $50-150

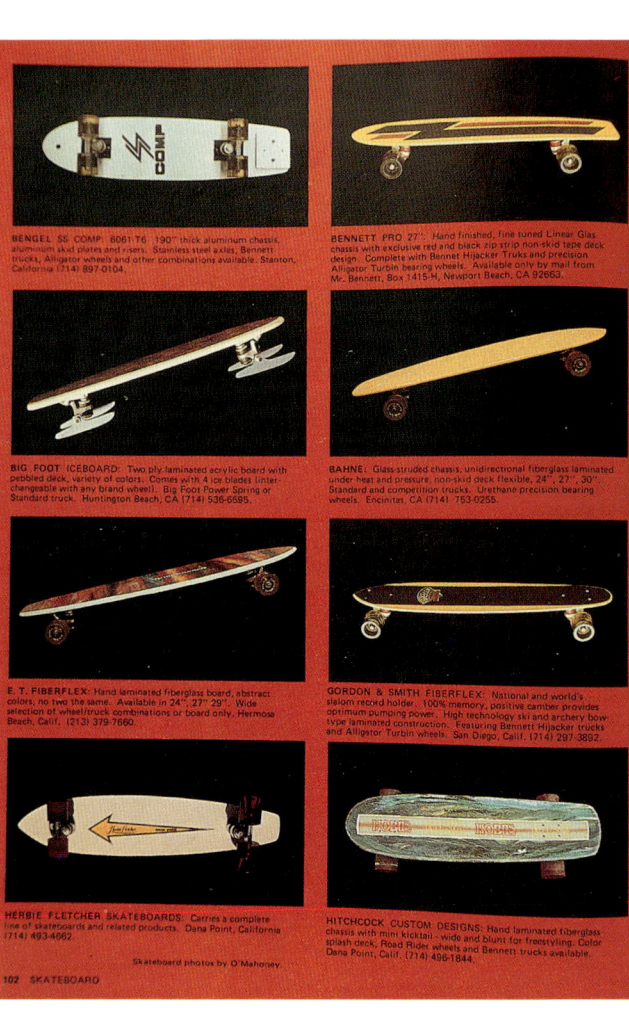

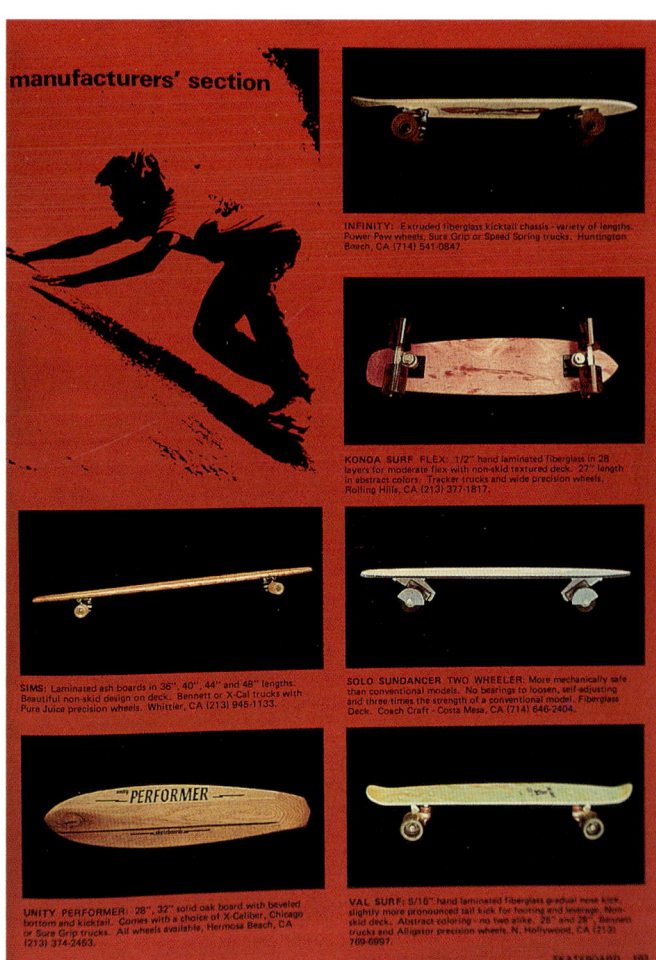

Product reviews from the *Skateboard Handbook.* Each of these boards are worth anywhere from $50-200, provided they are mounted with wheels and trucks. *Courtesy James O' Mahoney*

Ski Skate was designed for skating on grass. The Ski Skate was one of the many rare hybrids of the skateboarding industry. *Courtesy James O' Mahoney.*

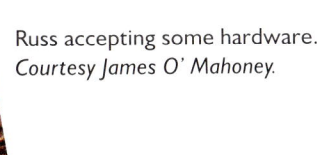

Russ accepting some hardware. *Courtesy James O' Mahoney.*

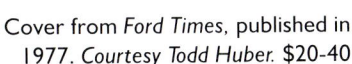

Cover from *Ford Times*, published in 1977. *Courtesy Todd Huber.* $20-40

Movie posters from *Skateboard*, the movie. Produced by Universal Studios in the 70s. *Courtesy Todd Huber.* $50-100

Val Surf ad out of the *Skateboard Handbook*. Courtesy James O'Mahoney.

Rare knee board. *Photo: Rhyn Noll*

Early Santa Cruz deck.

20 Years of Great Skateboarders

- **Tony Alva:** In 1977 Tony stepped into the forefront after winning world championships in Carlsbad Park.
- **Don "Waldo" Autry**: Mid-1970s pipe and pool riding, and extreme pipe skating in Arizona Desert.
- **Danny Bearer:** A member of the first place Hobie Super Surfer Team in the 1964 Anaheim Nationals, and Logan Earth Ski Team in 1975.
- **Dr. Ricky Blackhart:** In 1977 & 1978 he was the organizer of media events such as Catalina Classic and Free Former in Akron Ohio. He also was an early vert king.
- **John Freis:** A member of the Makaha and Hobie Super Surfer Teams. First place overall in 1965 Anaheim. Innovator of the nose wheelie.
- **Dave Hilton:** Youngest member of the Hobie Super Surfer Team. Made *Skateboarder*, Volume One.
- **Steve Hilton:** Older brother of Dave, also a member of Hobie team. He and his brother skated in Anaheim nationals in 1965.
- **Bruce Logan:** From 1964 to 1977 Bruce took first in over twenty-two contests. Some consider the Logans to be the First Family of Skateboarding. He skated in the Anaheim Nationals.
- **Bob Mohr:** Top free-styler of the 1970s. Bahne Team. Placed in the top four at Anaheim in 1965.
- **Ty Page:** Depicted on Blamo Bubble gum cards and did early kick flips. The public image of skateboarding reached new heights in 1977, thanks to Ty.
- **Nathan Pratt**: A member of the Zephyr team in 1975, and also played a role in the equipment advances in pool riding and downhill.
- **Laura Thornhill:** Took first place in the majority of the women's contests.
- **Gregg Weaver:** Cover of *Skateboarding*, Volume Two, #1. Emulated for his style in the '70s.
- **Chris Yandall:** First place Slalom in 1975 Bahne Cadillac nationals. Major slalom competitor in the 1970s.

Chapter 4

The 1980s

The 1980s started out with skateboarding's second slump. Legal wranglings over the safety of the sport and competition from other endeavors meant that only the truly dedicated hung with the sport.

In 1980 Steve Pezman, renamed *Skateboarder* magazine, which he had restarted in 1975 from the old *Skateboarder Quarterly*. The new magazine was symbolic of the times, featuring many different sports and changing its name to *Action Now*. It was published from August, 1980 until 1982. These are worth considerable amounts to collectors today.

The waning interest led to the tragic loss of almost all of the skate parks. Skateboarders were forced to go to their backyards, where they constructed homemade ramps. These ramps wood-framed construction with a plywood surface, sprouted up everywhere. On these surfaces new moves were put through the rigors: aerials, ollies, grinds and fakies.

Cover of *Skateboarder Magazine*, 1980. Most *Skateboarder* magazines are worth $40-80.

John Hudson at Laguna Seca races. *Courtesy Rich Novak and NHS. Photo: Piumarta.*

Rick "Spidey" doing a layback slide and roll in Alhambra, California, at Phills Ramp. *Courtesy Rich Novak and NHS. Photo: Keenan.*

Jeff Kendall riding one of his models. *Courtesy Rich Novak and NHS. Photo: Keenan.*

Rob Rosopp at the Lance Mountain Ramp with a front side invert. *Courtesy Rich Novak and NHS. Photo: Keenan.*

Jeff Kendall definitely catching some air! *Courtesy Rich Novak and NHS. Photo: Keenan.*

Though embattled, the sport did not die. In manufacturing Vision Skate Company was at the forefront of the 1980s. Rick and Peter Ducommun's Skull Skate emerged as a strong competitor in the early 1980s. Boards got lighter, wheels got smaller. Concave boards appeared. Standard board size in the 1980s was 10 x 30, made with 7-ply laminated maple. In 1981, *Thrasher* started its publication.

Competitions continued too. Roger Hickey won the Stand Up at the Glendora Mountain Race in 1980, and Jim Lad won the Lay Down Division. The Vans Off Shore Amateur Skate Finals were held in Del Mar. Tony Hawk was skating in the boys' age 11-13 division.

Duane Peters won the professional division at the Skate City Pro Am, while Lance Mountain took first in the amateur event.

In 1982 Tony Hawk won his first competition at Del Mar Skate Ranch. The Bones Brigade Skate Team began to take on shape, and would become a springboard for many young skate stars. Steve Caballero, Lance Mountain, Tommy Guerreo, Mike McGill, and Tony Hawk made up the team. They all remained a driving force in the 1980s.

Duane Peters with an early '80s grind. *Courtesy Rich Novak and NHS.*

Tony getting some back yard action. *Courtesy Jim Phillips.*

Things began to turn around in 1983. Skateboard organization like MESS (Mid Eastern Skateboard Series), CASL (California Amateur Skateboard League) began to pop up around the country. In 1983, *Transworld Skateboarding* started publication.

Jeff Kendall with some '80s air. *Courtesy Rich Novak and NHS.*

Rob Robskopp pool riding. *Courtesy Jim Phillips and NHS.*

In 1984 vert was king. The Hosoi Hammerhead skateboard was everywhere, and freestyle street skating followed. Jack Smith set out on his second journey across the country with fellow skaters Bob Denike, Paul Dunn, and Gary Fluitt. This time they crossed America in 26 days.

Powell Peralta and the Bones Brigade was a major influence in the mid-1980s. The first Bones Brigade Video was created by Stacy Peralta and Craig Stecyk, and sold 30,000 copies in 1985. Skateboarding regained its momentum.

Paul Schmitt, with Schmitt Sticks, moved into high gear, selling 50,000 boards a month. He hired Monty Nolder, the only deaf Pro Skater; he rode for Schmitt Sticks. Regional associations conglomerated into NSA (National Skateboarding Association), and neon clothing prevailed.

NHS produced the Bullet. *Courtesy Rich Novak and NHS.*

A collage of skaters. *Courtesy Rich Novak and NHS*

The Handplant. *Courtesy Rich Novak and NHS.*

In 1986, there were still slalom and high jump events in Vancouver, British Columbia, where the Transworld Skateboarding Championships were held. Bob Skoldberg took home the win.

Rob Roskopf. *Courtesy Rich Novak and NHS. Photo: Keenan*

Ramp grinding in the 1980s. *Courtesy Jim Phillips and NHS.*

In 1987, Powell Peralta produced *The Search for Animal Chin*, one of the first real skate films. This led to a whole stream of skate videos. Peralta, along with Vision, produced *Skate Vision* and *Psycho Skate,* featuring Rodney Mullen. Rodney was dubbed the king of freestyle, bringing new hype to the era.

Product photos left to right—Jeff Kendall, Claus Grabre, Jeff Grosso. These models, mounted up like this in mint condition, are worth $100-200. In ten years? *Courtesy Rich Novak and NHS.*

Strange Notes Magazine covers. *Courtesy Jim Phillips.*

This guy is getting some sick air in Japan. *Courtesy Rich Novak and NHS.*

During this time, Skip Engblom started Santa Monica Airlines Skate Company, while Steve Rocco, with the help of Rodney Mullen and Mike Valley, was responsible for creating World Industries. Pro skaters were moving into the business of building skateboards, which loosened the grip of the major manufacturers of the time.

Board from Santa Monica Airlines. $50-100, deck only.

Sergie Ventura flying high with a back side air at Tempe, Arizona. *Courtesy Rich Novak and NHS. Photo: Keenan.*

Christian Hosoi with his Indy Air in Tempe, Arizona. *Courtesy Rich Novak and NHS. Photo: Keenan.*

Lester Kasai in back side air.
Courtesy Jim Phillips, Rich Novak, and NHS. Photo: Keenan.

Lester Kasai cooling off at dusk with a front side air. Virginia Beach, Virginia. *Courtesy Rich Novak and NHS. Photo: Keenan.*

Rob Roskopp planting his foot in Chicago. *Courtesy Rich Novak and NHS. Photo: Keenan.*

Steve Alba front side grind, Laverne, California. *Courtesy Rich Novak and NHS. Photo: Keenan.*

Jeff Grosso at Tempe, Arizona. *Courtesy Rich Novak and NHS.*

Grosso with an Indy tap. *Courtesy Rich Novak and NHS. Photo Keenan*

Steve Alba's back yard tail tap in Laverne, California. *Courtesy Jim Phillips.*

John Gibson laying back and rolling out. *Courtesy Rich Novak and NHS. Photo: Keenan.*

Jeff Kendall with a layback air. *Courtesy Rich Novak and NHS. Photo: Keenan.*

Steve Caballero, Virginia Beach, Virginia, doing a sad plant. *Courtesy Rich Novak and NHS. Photo: Keenan.*

Rob Roskopp with a crowd of onlookers. *Courtesy Rich Novak and NHS. Photo: Keenan.*

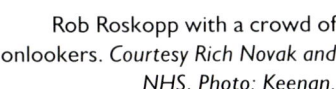

Eric Castro in Alhambra, California, having a street ramp session. *Courtesy Rich Novak and NHS. Photo: Keenan.*

Jeff Kendall with some mid-1980s air. *Courtesy Rich Novak and NHS. Photo: Keenan*

Skater catching air in the mid 1980s. *Courtesy Rich Novak and NHS. Photo: Keenan*

By 1988, the third wave of skateboarding popularity was upon us. Television events spotlighted vertical ramp skating. *Gleaming the Cube* is made, kind of a rock and roll skate flick. Powell Peralta released its fourth video, called *The Public Domain*. The Pipeline in Upland closed.

Jason Jessee. *Courtesy Rich Novak and NHS. Photo: Keenan.*

This is what an average shop in the '80s looked like. *Courtesy Rich Novak and NHS.*

Chuck Dinkins with a pressure air. *Courtesy Rich Novak and NHS.*

The 1980s were a decade of maturation and experimentation. The skate industry was in heavy competition and seemed to have taken on a mind of it own. Companies battled for position. Pools, ramps, vert, and air moves cre- ated in the 1970s were refined in the 1980s. Serious design innovations increased board performance, and aerial moves gave rise to stalled inverts and the vertical 540 slide. Flight was achieved by man for the second time this century!

Brian Pennington catching some crisp air. *Courtesy Rich Novak and NHS.*

Rob Mertz in Huston, Texas. *Courtesy Jim Phillips, Rich Novak, and NHS.*

These guys leave the 1980s with aerial style.
Courtesy Jim Phillips, Rich Novak, and NHS.

In 1988 Christian Hosoi won Vision Skate Escape. Allen Gelfand won the highest air in the first Big O contest. Steve Olson won the overall prize. Steve Hirsch, Eddie Elguera, Allen Losi, Ray Rodriguez, Duane Peters, Mickey Alba, all placed in the Big O, and many more, too numerous to mention, were the stoke in the 1980s.

Vert was the word for the late 1980s. Knees were torn learning how to fall, but vert continued. Pools, pipes, and spill ways became concrete waves to ride. Among the pioneers were Steve Olson and Steve Alba who excelled at pipe skating.

Steve Alba pipe skating. *Courtesy Rich Novak and NHS. Photo: Keenan.*

Steve Alba at the Upland Pipeline. *Courtesy Rich Novak and NHS. Photo: Keenan.*

Steve Alba with his front side grind at a pool in Palm Springs, that is a nudist colony. *Courtesy Rich Novak and NHS. Photo: Keenan.*

127

Mickey Alba in the Upland Pipeline. *Courtesy Rich Novak and NHS. Photo: Keenan.*

Steve Alba rimming a pool. *Courtesy Rich Novak and NHS.*

Nicke Alba going beyond vert. *Courtesy Rich Novak and NHS. Photo: Keenan.*

Foot plant off the stairs. *Courtesy Jim Phillips, Rich Novak, and NHS.*

The machine-driven pro skate world wasn't stopping for anything now. When it comes to individualistic behavior, skaters had cornered the market since the early 1960s.

Accessories were abundant in the 1980s. *Courtesy Jim Phillips, Rich Novak, and NHS.*

Steve Alba pipe skating in Upland, California.
Courtesy Rich Novak and NHS. Photo: Keenan.

In 1989 skateboarding progressed with radical leaps and bounds. Downhill luging surfaced and gained momentum. Everyone seemed to take credit for some variation of a trick and everybody took responsibility to give them all names. The favorite terrains for skating were plazas and school yards, and the Embarcadero in San Francisco was a skateboard Mecca. Back in Anaheim, the NSA Vans Factory contest was won by Chris Miller.

Bod Boyle with some high-altitude skating. *Courtesy Rich Novak and NHS. Photo: Keenan*

Ross Goodman in a San Jose warehouse. *Courtesy Rich Novak and NHS. Photo: Kobata.*

LEFT: Bod Boyle planting at Cooleys Ramp. *Courtesy Jim Phillips, Rich Novak, and NHS. Photo: Keenan*

RIGHT: Eric Dressen gliding down a stair rail. *Courtesy Rich Novak and NHS. Photo Roberts*

Vertical superstars of the 1980s were Tony Hawk, Steve Caballero, Christian Hosoi, Danny Way, Colin McKay, Bucky Lasek, Mickey and Steve Alba, Mike McGill, Mike Smith, John Lucero, Jim Gray, Neil Blender, Eddie Reatigui, Dave Duncan, Mark Gator Rogowski, Steve Olson, and Duane Peters. Other 1980 legends were Neil Blender, Eric Dressen, Kevin Harris, Mark Gonzales, Tommy Guerrero, John Lucero, Rodney Mullen, Natas Kaupas, Lance Mountain, Jeff Phillips, Rob Roskopp, Mike Valley,

Product photos of 1980 boards. *Courtesy Jim Phillips.* $50-150, deck only.

The Duane Peters model. *Courtesy Rich Novak and NHS.* $50-150

1980s boards. *Courtesy Todd Huber. Photo: Rhyn Noll.* $50-150

Some 1989 grinds that hint at things to come. *Courtesy Jim Phillips.*

1989 product photos, at the doorstep of the next decade. The graphics and signature boards of this era are definitely what makes these boards collectable. Their condition is critical. *Courtesy Jim Phillips, Rich Novak, and NHS.*

A group of boards from 1980, some of which are sure to be collectible. *Courtesy Skip Egblom. Photos by Rhyn Noll.* $50-150, deck only.

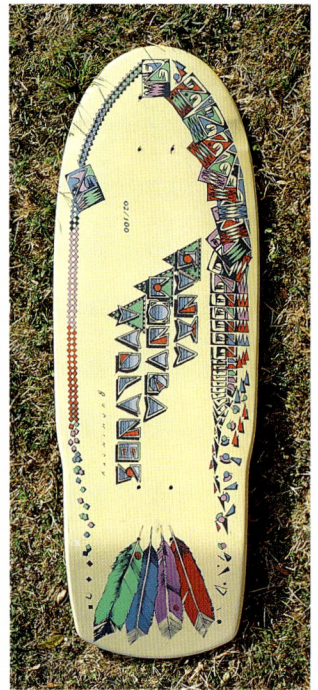

Cory O'Brien Pro Model, Santa Cruz, 1989. *Courtesy Rich Novak and NHS*. $50-150, deck only.

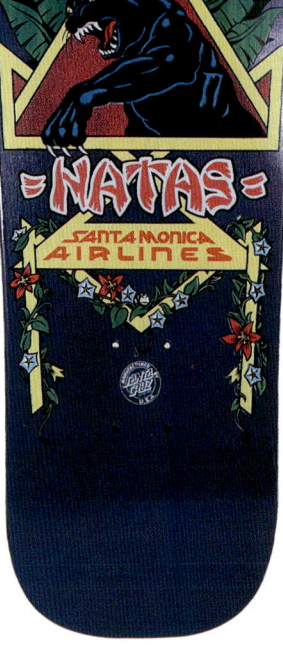

Natas model from Santa Monica Airlines. *Courtesy Jim Phillips*. $50-150, deck only.

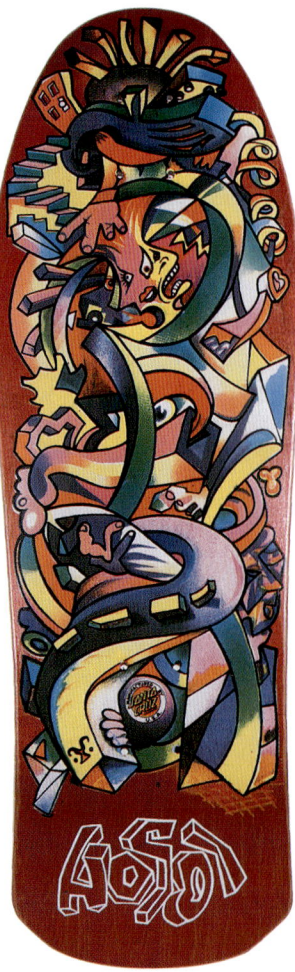

Rob Roskoff Screaming Face, 1986. *Courtesy Jim Phillips*. $50-150, deck only.

Christian Hosoi pro model, 1989. *Courtesy Jim Phillips*. $50-150, deck only.

Jeff Kendall pro model, 1986. *Courtesy Jim Phillips*. $50-150, deck only.

1986 OJ Team Rider wheel. *Courtesy Jim Phillips.*

Skateboards from the 1980s in the Skate Lab Museum. *Courtesy Todd Huber. Photo: Rhyn Noll*

The transition leading into the '90s.
Courtesy Rich Novak and NHS.

The 1980s Independent truck style has a springloaded axle for suspension. *Courtesy Rich Novak and NHS. Photo: Rhyn Noll.*

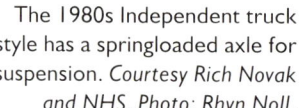

Chapter 5
The 1990s

• 1990: The Berlin wall collapsed, and the Cold War as we knew it ended.

The early 1990s showed a decline in vert skating, creating strain for the skateboarding industry. They were subject to the general perceptions of society, and negative attitudes and a recession affected skateboards' popularity for the third time. This was short-lived, though.

Courtesy Rich Novak and NHS.

Razor Dressen. *Courtesy Rich Novak and NHS.*

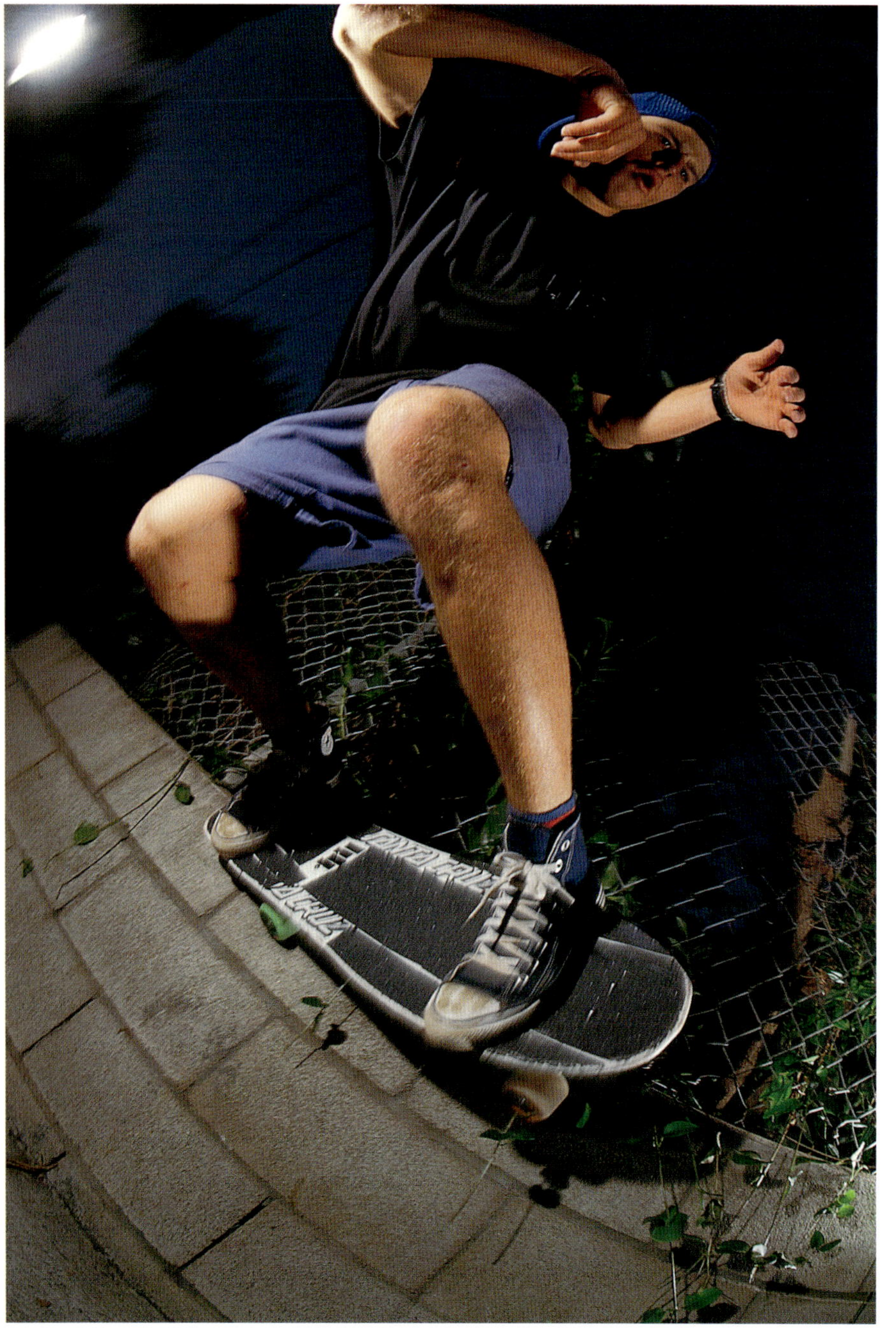

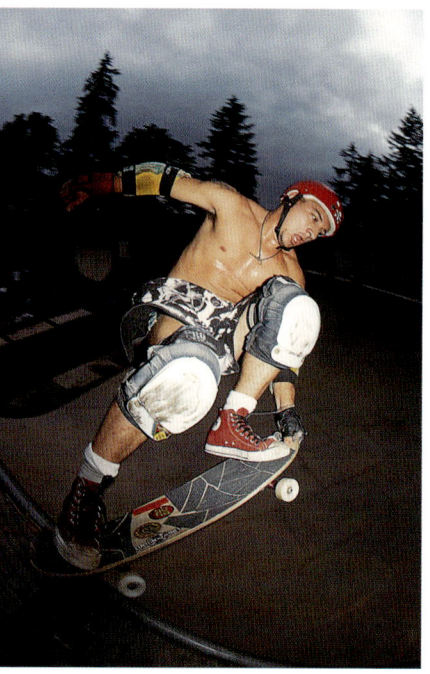

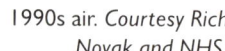

Jason Jesse. *Courtesy Jim Phillips, Rich Novak, and NHS.*

Steve Alba. *Courtesy Rich Novak and NHS Photo: Keenan*

1990s air. *Courtesy Rich Novak and NHS.*

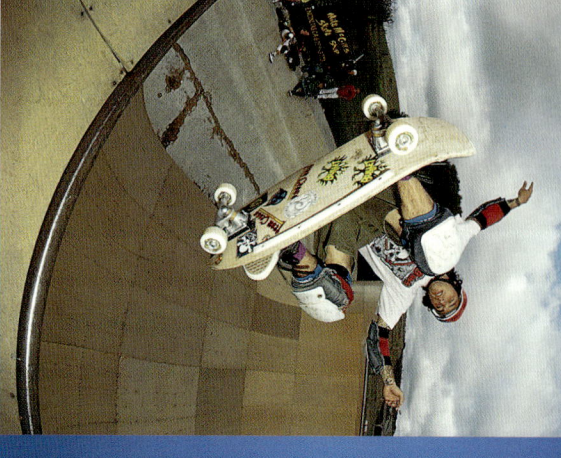

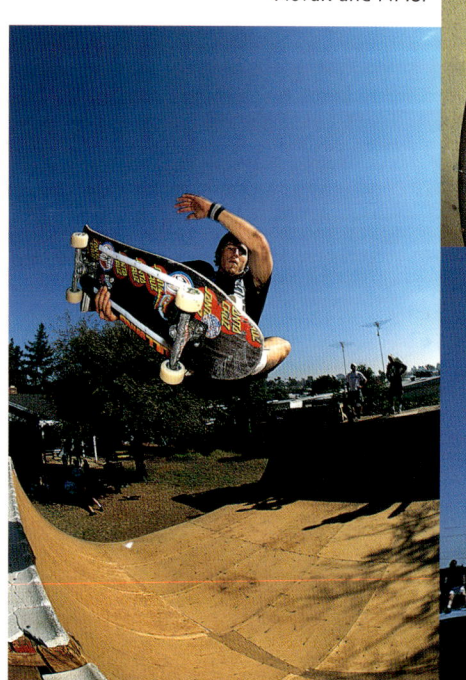

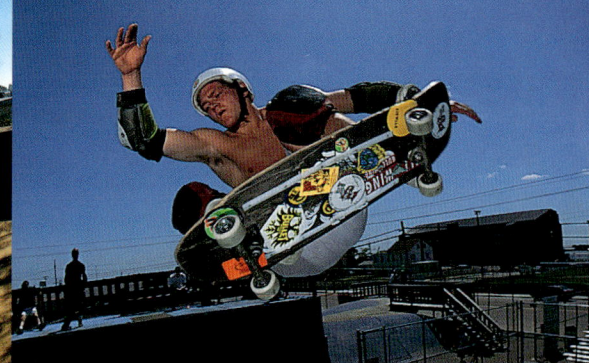

5-foot longboard by Noll Streetsurfer. 13-ply, Baltic Birch. *Courtesy Streetsurfer Co.* $150-250, mounted.

50-inch gun design by Noll Streetsurfer. 11 ply, Baltic Birch. *Courtesy Street Surfer Co.* $100-200, mounted.

Early 1990s boards. Mounted with wheels and trucks, $50-200. *Courtesy Skip Engblom.*

Early 1990s boards. Mounted with wheels and trucks, $50-200. *Courtesy Rich Novak and NHS.*

Jim Phillips, a famous rock artist, has created art for noted artists such as Neil Young, Willie Nelson, and the Doors. As early as 1976 Jim's art was also influencing skate graphics at Santa Cruz Skateboards. Most of the notable graphics on Santa Cruz skateboards are his work. He has remained in touch through NHS Pro Riders and his son Jimbo. I believe that the art and graphics are one of the elements that makes a board collectible. Jim now works on snowboard graphics for NHS.

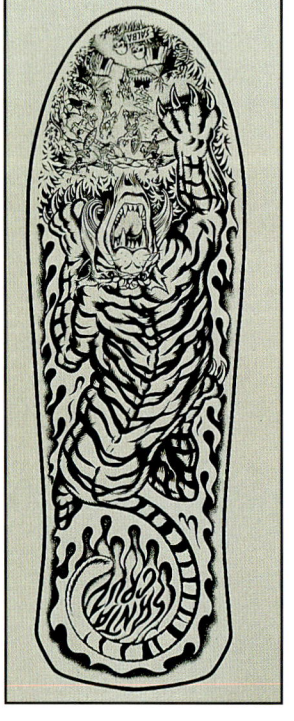

There seems to be a direct correlation between drought years and skating popularity. It seems that when pools and spillways dried out, skaters moved in. Perhaps the lack of surf during these dry spells contributed to skating popularity. ESPN and network TV gave ultimate exposure to skating. In 1991 Stacy Peralta left the Powell Corporation.

Pat Ngoho in Los Angeles.
Courtesy Jim Phillips, Rich Novak, and NHS.

The concave board was created and boards got stronger with better function. A deep concave might flick and rotate well, but if the rider can't feel the board because only the heel and toe are touching, it will affect the ride. A middle of the road board seems to be best, not too concave extreme and not too flat.

Riding vertical and upward remained the direction of choice with the freestylers of skating. Guys put wax and even soap on the bottom for lubrication, and better grinds. Hard wheels provided necessary durability and reduced grip for easier grinds; the trade-off was a rough ride. These wheels apply in vert, a softer wheel provided a softer ride. On the street and in jump skating, a whole array of grinds and airs were used. Many of the old-school tricks had been forgotten by freestylers, but the range of tricks could go on forever—grinds, curb rail, air moves of all kinds, including flips—whatever's available. These characteristics dominated this era.

Bob Boyle. *Courtesy Jim Phillips, Rich Novak, and NHS.*

A demonstration of "flick" in motion. *Photo: Rhyn Noll.*

During my fact-finding mission I ran across a kid in Ventura. Dial 1-800-ten-toes. J.D. Stites demonstrates extreme finesse with this pipe grind and flick. *Photo: Rhyn Noll*

OJ Wheels. *Courtesy Rich Novak and NHS.*

Chet Childress. *Courtesy Rich Novak and NHS. Photo: Lance Dalgart*

1992 *Big Brother* magazine began, started by Steve Rocco, and was later sold to Larry Flynt, and Sonja Catalano creates the Professional Skateboard League.

Big Brother magazine, 50th issue, July 1999.

•1990s: The rise of the internet creates an expanded network of information.

The normal kid still found a huge gap between what he could achieve and what the pros were achieving. Double kicks and concaves prevailed in the freestyle street skating realm, which still dominated.

Longboard skateboarding resurfaced in the early 1990s and grew. The first longboards to resurface included Tops, Weber, Sector 9, Gravity, and The Noll Streetsurfer™. Alternative boards began to appear everywhere! In the early 1990s surfboard builders tried to regain control of the product they gave birth to. Through thick and thin, surfers have nurtured the idea of board sports.

In 1994, the National Skateboarding Association, run by Frank Hawk, closed its doors.

Skateboarding's exposure continued to expand. There were skateboard magazines in virtually every country on the planet, even Russia, including four in the USA—*Big Brother, Slap, Thrasher,* and *Transworld Skateboarding.* Skate videos also help to spread skating's popularity.

In 1995, ESPN started the Extreme Games, featuring skateboarding. The fourth wave of popularity is here. The video *Welcome to Hell* is released by Toy Machine.

Dino Miranda in Hawaii above Waimea. Notice his hand brakes. *Courtesy Streetsurfer Co. Photo: Rhyn Noll.*

Buttons and child.
Courtesy Gravity.

Buttons Kaluhiokalani at 8 Banks.
Courtesy Gravity. Photo: Steve Sherman

C.J. Nelson socks in with poise
and style. *Photo: Patrick Trefz*

Buttons in the 1990s. *Photo Patrick Trefz.*

Rhyn Noll, drop knee in Nor Cal.
Courtesy Streetsurfer Co. Photo: Sarah Campbell.

Skateboard deck, undrilled and in a pristene state, for decorative purposes. $400. *Courtesy of Noll Streetsurfer.*

Shylo Steinthal skating down the boardwalk in Wesport, Washington. *Courtesy Streetsurfer Co. Photo: Rhyn Noll.*

Road Rider Wheels. *Courtesy Rich Novak and NHS.*

Tom Wegener in Solana Beach. *Courtesy Gravity. Photo: Steve Sherman*

The Bullet, by Santa Cruz. *Courtesy Jim Phillips, Rich Novak, and NHS.* $50-150

Art Godoy. *Courtesy Rich Novak and NHS.*

1990s boards, $50-150 if mounted with wheels and trucks. *Courtesy Jim Phillips, Rich Novak, and NHS.*

Air in the orchard. *Courtesy Jim Phillips, Rich Novak, and NHS.*

Duane Peters, poolside. *Courtesy Rich Novak and NHS. Photo: Putnam*

With the help of Jim Fitzpatrick, California passed law AB1296 that restricts "sue-happy individuals from injuring themselves and then trying to blame somebody else" for their misfortune.

The 1990s saw a regrouping of the people who grew up with the sport. The choices in types of skating returned as more women and kids were skating than ever before. These included hi-flying, tricks, cruising, carving, downhill, traditional skating, street skating, and many others. As skateboarders attempted to get back what they had lost through the evolution of the skateboard, longboards resurfaced and there was a return to more traditional moves out of the early days of skateboarding. Everything seemed to come full circle, but at the same time, it was new and alien to an industry that had focused on vert and air for two decades.

A myriad of stickers. *Courtesy Jim Phillips, Rich Novak, and NHS.*

Steve Smith with a nose wheelie. Background: Point St. George Lighthouse mural, Crescent City, California. *Courtesy Street Surfer Co. Photo: Rhyn Noll.*

Bank Slide. *Courtesy Gravity.*

Steve Smith and Paul Valley contemplate this tree's history, which stretches way beyond skateboarding's history. In fact these trees have been growing for thousands of years. *Courtesy Streetsurfer Co. Photo: Rhyn Noll*

Rhyn Noll. *Courtesy Streetsurfer Co. Photo: Sarah Campbell*

Brad Edwards at Baldy Pipe. *Courtesy Gravity. Photo: Ron Lemen*

Dino Miranda cruising in Hawaii. *Courtesy Street Surfer Co. Photo: Rhyn Noll*

With the new longboard companies, a new market was created. It was not mainstream and that's the way most longboarders liked it. This seems to have given anyone with access to veneer potential to be a skateboard company. More than forty longboard companies had popped up by the late 1990s Even large skate companies that had before produced only freestylers are now building "longboards." Companies that went out of business in the 1970s, like Makaha and Fiberflex, were reborn. Hard or soft, small or big, it was your choice in the 1990s

The 1990s are known as the decade that "skateboarding became self-aware" and returned to its roots. Freestyle skaters of the 1990s flew higher and got radder than ever before. They pushed the sport to new heights. Thanks to advancements in photography, skate images of this era were unparalleled in previous decades. At this time, large freestyle skate companies still dominated the industry.

Jessica Bishop at Seaside. *Courtesy Gravity. Photo: Steve Sherman*

Courtesy Gravity.

Veronica Kay in Santa Cruz. *Courtesy Gravity. Photo: Steve Sherman*

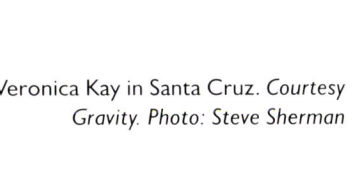

Remy Noll skating with style and grace with five over. *Courtesy Streetsurfer Co. Photo: Rhyn Noll*

Dane Noll showing how easy it is to ride longboard. *Courtesy Streetsurfer Co. Photo: Rhyn Noll*

Remy Noll cruising at twilight. *Courtesy Streetsurfer Co. Photo: Rhyn Noll*

From left to right Remy Noll, Dane Noll, and Nick with boards almost as tall as they are. *Courtesy Streetsurfer Co. Photo: Rhyn Noll.*

TOP LEFT: Kids of each era skating. These are the great shots. *Courtesy Streetsurfer Co. Photo: Rhyn Noll.*

TOP CENTER: Steve Smith at the airport. *Courtesy Streetsurfer Co. Photo: Rhyn Noll*

BOTTOM : *Courtesy Gravity*

Michael Bream at 8 Banks. *Courtesy Gravity. Photo. Steve Sherman*

Gravity Skate Team.
Courtesy Gravity.

Brad Edwards at the Nude Bowl, doing a frontside grind. *Courtesy Gravity. Photo: Michael Bream*

Rhyn Noll five over the nose wheelie. *Courtesy Streetsurfer Co. Photo: Sarah Campbell.*

Steve Smith riding on the edge of space in Arcata, California. *Photo: Rhyn Noll*

Brad Edwards at Henshaw Dam. *Courtesy Gravity. Photo: Michael Bream*

Street Surfer Team Photos stretching back to 1996. Team photos say a lot about a particular time and feel of the people and place. *Courtesy Street Surfer Co. Photos: Patrick Trefz and Rhyn Noll*

Rhyn Noll. *Courtesy Streetsurfer Co. Photo: Sarah Campbell*

Remy Noll with a ghostly grab rail. *Courtesy Streetsurfer Co. Photo: Rhyn Noll.*

PARKING IN REAR

DRIV

165

What is collectible from the 1990s? Skateboard graphics, as well as unique signed and numbered exotic wood boards. All things become collectible over time. The trick is to understand why; consider quality, quantity, rarity, historical value, condition, and uniqueness. There are some small companies that have arisen in the 1990s that have taken notice of the collectibility of a skateboard, including the Russ K Koa Longboard Company, Noll Streetsurfer Company with its original and replicas, and Gravity, who has a Longboard with a speedometer that looks promising.

Downhill Skater. *Courtesy Gravity.*

Gravity product photo. *Courtesy Gravity Skate Co.*

Rhyn Noll. Location: airport. *Courtesy Streetsurfer Co. Photo: Sarah Campbell.*

Steve Smith, Nor Cal tripod. *Courtesy Streetsurfer Co. Photo: Rhyn Noll*

Setup for longboard in the 1990s. *Courtesy Streetsurfer Co. Photo: Rhyn Noll.*

Rob Israel at sunset on a 21-inch board. *Courtesy Street Surfer Co. Photo: Rhyn Noll*

Steve Smith. *Courtesy Street Surfer Co. Photo: Rhyn Noll*

Jeff Catalano in Pacific Beach. *Courtesy Gravity. Photo: Steve Sherman*

Dane Noll showing the relationship between skate and surf, ducking under a curtain of liquid light. *Courtesy Streetsurfer Co. Photo: Rhyn Noll*

Paul Valley with the sky grind in Humboldt County. *Courtesy Streetsurfer Co. Photo: Rhyn Noll*

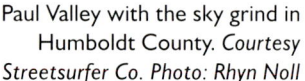

Steve Smith, with a backwards nose wheelie. *Courtesy Streetsurfer Co. Photo: Rhyn Noll*

Cover of *International Longboarder* magazine, Vol. 1, 1999.

Shylo Steinthall with a nose wheelie on Roy Avenue. *Courtesy Shylo Steinthall.*

Mounted longboard, Street Surfer, 4 feet long. *Courtesy Streetsurfer Co. Photo: Rhyn Noll.* $200

I rode a steel-wheeled hot dogger around one day and realized why they were a terror in the 1960s. The noise and vibration is high, and just pulling a turn is rad! *Photo: Sarah Campbell*

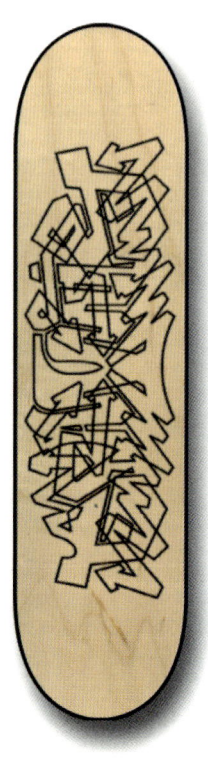

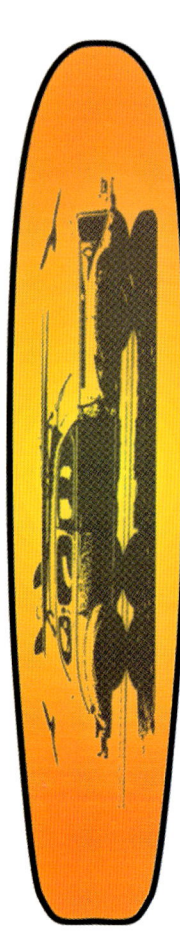

Rare handpainted skate-
board replica, $400-500.
Courtesy Streetsurfer Co.
Photo: Rhyn Noll.

Courtesy Gravity. $50-200

36" skateboard. *Courtesy Streetsurfer Co. Photo: Rhyn Noll. $50-100, deck only.*

When you walk in to Skate Lab this is what you see.
Courtesy Todd Huber. Photo: Rhyn Noll

PowerPly deck, 1998. *Courtesy Rich Novak and NHS. Photo: Justin McIvor* $50-100

These are just some of NHS's hot boards in the 1990s. *Photo: Rhyn Noll. Courtesy Rich Novak and NHS.* $50-80, deck only.

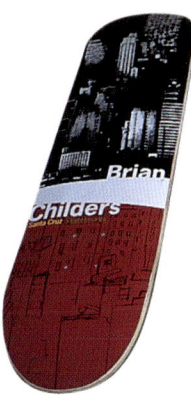
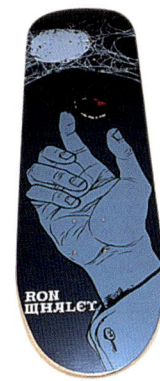

Profile of a 1990s skateboard. *Courtesy Jim Phillips, Rich Novak, and NHS.*

The Duke room. Courtesy Ed Economy. *Photo: Rhyn Noll.*

NHS Factory. Men at work, designing the next collectible graphic. *Photo: Rhyn Noll*

This Birds Eye 48-inch longboard is one of two known to exist. *Courtesy Street Surfer Co.* $500-600. *Photo: Rhyn Noll*

Collectible Jackets. *Courtesy Tom Craig.* $50-200. *Photo: Rhyn Noll*

Tom Craig, along with other great old school skaters, have managed to hang onto a piece of the sport's history. *Courtesy Tom Craig. Photo: Rhyn Noll*

Rare scooters from A to Z at the Skate Lab Museum. *Courtesy Todd Huber. Photo: Rhyn Noll*

This could be a perfect example of a board that is going to become collectible. *Courtesy Skip Engblom. Photo: Rhyn Noll*

Other boards in Tom Craig's collection. *Photo: Rhyn Noll. Courtesy Tom Craig.*

**OPPOSITE PAGE:
LEFT to RIGHT:**

48-inch longboard by Street Surfer Company. $50-200. *Photo: Rhyn Noll*

Double kick 48-inch longboard by Street Surfer Co. $50-200. *Photo: Rhyn Noll*

37-inch Double Kick designed for park riding by Street Surfer Co. $50-150. *Photo: Rhyn Noll*

33-inch Double Kick Double Concave by Street Surfer Company. $50-150. *Photo: Rhyn Noll*

48-inch winged longboard by Boris. Mounted with wheels and trucks, $50-150. *Photo: Rhyn Noll*

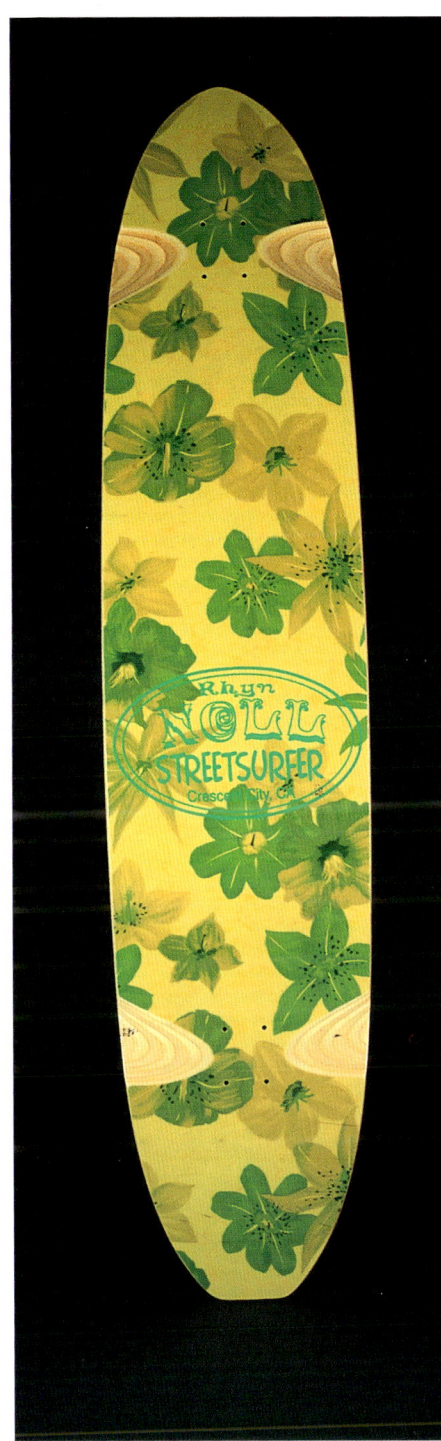

This is the board John Hudson used at Laguna Seca in the Downhill. *Courtesy Rich Novak and NHS. Photo: Rhyn Noll*

Product photos of laminated wood surfboard-like skateboards. 4- and 5-footers. *Courtesy Street Surfer Co. Photo: Rhyn Noll.* $250-400

A small skate factory. *Courtesy Street Surfer Company. Photo: Rhyn Noll*

Other rare collectibles at the Skate Lab Museum. *Courtesy Todd Huber. Photo: Rhyn Noll*

My collection. *Photo: Gary Holley*

Poster wall in Skate Lab Museum. *Courtesy Todd Huber. Photo: Rhyn Noll*

Books on skateboarding in the Skate Lab Museum. *Courtesy Todd Huber. Photo: Rhyn Noll*

A wall dedicated to Skate Magazines. *Courtesy Todd Huber. Photo: Rhyn Noll.*

Skate collection at Skatelab Skatepark and Museum. *Courtesy Todd Huber. Photo: Rhyn Noll.*

A glimpse into a collector's garage. *Courtesy Ed Economy. Photo: Rhyn Noll.*

Randy Beck with some of his collection at his shop in Chadsworth. *Photo: Rhyn Noll.*

Evidence of the sport's true place in culture came in 1997 when the U.S. Postal Service released a skateboarding stamp. Miniature skateboards were also introduced in the 1990s.

Miniature skateboard.
Photo: Rhyn Noll

Steve Smith grinding rusty rail. *Courtesy Street Surfer Co. Photo: Rhyn Noll*

Hand plant at the Skate Lab Pool.
Courtesy Todd Huber. Photo: Rhyn Noll.

Kirly. *Courtesy Rich Novak and NHS. Photo: Lance Dalgart*

Jake Jones. *Courtesy Rich Novak and NHS. Photo: Lance Dalgart*

Joe Hutchison. *Courtesy Rich Novak and NHS. Photo: Aaron Jones*

Tim Brauch. *Courtesy Rich Novak and NHS. Photo: Lance Dalgart*

Justin Strubing at a skate demo in Aptos, California. *Photo: Patrick Trefz*

Israel Fordes in Minneapolis, Minnesota. *Courtesy Rich Novak and NHS. Photo: John Humphries*

Sam Hitz. *Courtesy Rich Novak and NHS. Photo: Lance Dalgart*

Brian Childers. *Courtesy Rich Novak and NHS. Photo: Lance Dalgart*

Richard Kirby. *Courtesy Rich Novak and NHS. Photo: Lance Dalgart*

Chet Childress. *Courtesy Rich Novak and NHS. Photo: Lance Dalgart*

Brian Childers. *Courtesy Rich Novak and NHS. Photo: Lance Dalgart*

Mako Urabe. *Courtesy Rich Novak and NHS. Photo: Lance Dalgart*

Darren Navarrette. *Courtesy Rich Novak and NHS. Photo: Lance Dalgart*

Doug Shoemaker with what I call the "Impress Grind". *Courtesy Rich Novak and NHS. Photo: Lance Dalgart*

Tim Brauch. *Courtesy Rich Novak and NHS. Photo: Lance Dalgart*

Ron Whaley. *Courtesy Rich Novak and NHS. Photo: Brian Uydea*

Tim Brauch. *Courtesy Rich Novak and NHS. Photo: Lance Dalgart*

Tim Brauch. *Courtesy Rich Novak and NHS. Photo: Lance Dalgart*

Vanikhacobian. *Courtesy Rich Novak and NHS Photo: Lance Dalgart*

Dane Noll learning board flips at 7 years old. *Courtesy Streetsurfer Co. Photo: Rhyn Noll*

Chet Childress at the deep end. *Courtesy Rich Novak and NHS. Photo: Pete Thompson*

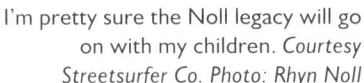
Richard Kirby. *Courtesy Rich Novak and NHS. Photo: Lance Dalgart*

I'm pretty sure the Noll legacy will go on with my children. *Courtesy Streetsurfer Co. Photo: Rhyn Noll*

Steve Smith traveling through urban areas; nothing stands in his way. *Courtesy Streetsurfer Co. Photo: Rhyn Noll*

Ollie over anything and everything. *Courtesy Streetsurfer Co. Photo: Rhyn Noll*

Republic Rider. *Courtesy Republic Co. Photo: Rhyn Noll.*

Republic Rider. *Courtesy Republic Co. Photo: Rhyn Noll*

Republic Skate Team and my son, Dane Noll. *Courtesy Republic Co. Photo: Rhyn Noll*

Night grinds. *Courtesy Rich Novak and NHS.*

By 1999, there was an estimated 9.3 million skateboarders just in the USA. Tony Hawk pulled the first 900 in history in the X-Games in San Francisco. It was definitely a milestone—basically two and a half revolutions in the air! Tony Hawk is to skateboarding what Micheal Jordan is to basketball. Tony retired on M.T.V. in 1999.

Jeff Budro at Encinitas YMCA, doing a melon grab over the hip. *Courtesy Gravity. Photo: Jarrod Tallman*

James Holmes at Encinitas YMCA, doing a melon tweak. *Courtesy Gravity. Photo: Michael Bream*

Josh Connerley at Encinitas YMCA, doing a frontside ollie. *Courtesy Gravity. Photo: Jarrod Tallman*

Dustin Taylor in San Diego, doing a frontside boardslide. *Courtesy Gravity. Photo: Jarrod Tallman*

Jeff Budro at Encinitas YMCA, doing an invert. *Courtesy Gravity. Photo: Michael Bream*

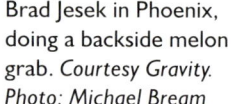

Brad Jesek in Phoenix, doing a backside melon grab. *Courtesy Gravity. Photo: Michael Bream*

Jeff Budro at Kelly's Pool, doing an invert. *Courtesy Gravity. Photo: Michael Bream*

Josh Connerley at Encinitas YMCA, doing a Shuvit. *Courtesy Gravity. Photo: Michael Bream*

Wheeled sports gained new respect in general, with a new found place in society. The 1999 Gravity Games, held in Providence, Rhode Island, gave new meaning to skateboarding, with mid-air technical maneuvers taking center stage. Bob Burnquist took the gold in vert. Buckey Lasek took second, Andy MacDonald third, and Tony Hawk fourth. I'm not sure if the overall standings meant a lot, because these guys are all Picassos of their art. Biker Sherlock won the gold in the stand-up downhill at the Gravity Games.

Watching the games really gave me a super stoke, not just because ramp skating has moved into a different realm, but because there was a more complete coverage of skateboarding as an established sport. This gave skaters worldwide a sense of satisfaction; we don't get the big money yet, but we are getting closer. Some say skateboarding is accepted into mainstream society, but I am not so sure. Ball sports still oversaturate my TV.

Switch Stance is the leading edge of vert in the late 1990s. This era is seeing a rebirth of skate parks, and these parks are exploding all over the world. Facilitation is good for kids and promoters; connections can be made. Kids, pros, and family can go participate in the interest of our youth on concrete or plywood waves.

Our forefathers generated the style of the 1960s and 1970s, in skateboarding's heyday. Going back to 1979 and 1980, we saw a total change in attitudes and style. There was much innovation in the 1980s and 1990s Today the common link between street, freestyle, and grass roots skaters is our history and the skateboard. Longboard skateboards have diversified the sport, and now everybody can find a skateboard style that is right for them. A new style of skating is evolving with its early ocean origins in the forefront.

Skateboarding is not going away. It is here for good. It is ingrained in America's culture and it is evolving in spurts decade by decade. I think we are on the doorstep of big changes beyond the 1990s

Courtesy Gravity.

Courtesy Gravity.

Skateparks are still crude in some smaller towns. Crescent City, California.
Photo: Rhyn Noll.

BELOW:
Overview of the skatepark in Arcata, California.
Photo: Rhyn Noll

191

The Men Who Make The Machines

Rich Novak is responsible in part for a certain stabilization to the industry, establishing price structures. He founded NHS in 1972, with **Doug Haut** and **Jay Shurman**, but Rich has been in the business since 1958. With Jay Shurman, Rich kicked off Independent Trucks. The two were longtime partners in the industry. Rich was involved with *Thrasher* Magazine and helped get the magazine off the ground after all other skate magazines disappeared in 1980. Rich says freestylists have taken over the industry in the 1990s Together, **Dave Dominy** and Rich are responsible for laminated hardwood decks, Santa Cruz Skateboards. Rich is also responsible for the Road Rider Wheel and both Alba Concave and O.J. wheels. He is a skateboard manufacturer of the highest caliber, and a businessman in the truest sense. NHS is the longest-running skate factory to date.

NHS has been collecting and hanging boards up since they began in 1975. These are just some of the thousands of boards they produced. Not often do we get to see the inner workings of a major skate factory; here is a rare glimpse inside. *Courtesy Rich Novak and NHS. Photo: Rhyn Noll*

Rich Novak, leader of NHS.
Photo: Rhyn Noll

Skip Engblom, 51 years old, was the first to be inducted into the Skateboard Hall of Fame. He started skating in 1958 in Hollywood, California on wooden wheels, which he says came before clay on Hollywood and Sunset. Skip is responsible for branding the logo on the 1960s Phil Edwards Model by Makaha. He was a major player in creating the Zephyr Skate Team in the late 1970s. He also started Santa Monica Airlines, and literally designed his boards to fly. Working in a surfboard factory he has been creating unique skateboards since the late fifties. Skip has a need to go back to the basics, paying tribute to this sport's beginning. Skip still skates; now he rides a four-foot longboard skateboard. Santa Monica Airlines closed its doors in 1981, but he is still involved in building skateboards today.

Skip Engblom. *Courtesy Skip Engblom.*

Courtesy Skip Engblom.

Skip Engblom in Santa Monica. *Photo: Rhyn Noll.*

Steve Rocco is a freestyle skater who was most instrumental in changing the industry in the 1980s and 1990s He helped get Santa Monica Airlines off the ground, and later created World Industries and Blind in the 1990s. He also started *Big Brother* magazine.

Tim Puimarta was an early team rider for Road Rider, and works for NHS today. He is a major player in design and manufacturing.

Frank Nasworthy (known as the Cadillac King, and considered by some to be the father of modern skating) and **Bill and Bob Bahne** were responsible for Cadillac wheels.

Craig Stecyk designed the Rat Bones logo for Powell Peralta, and is involved in filmmaking and photography. He skated on the Zephyr skate team.

Collectors

Dale Smith built skateboards in 1958 with the help of **Carson Hubbard**. You can always get a perspective of early skateboarding by talking with Dale; he knows as much as anybody about the early eras. He first started skating in 1958. When roots are considered, Dale is a wise old oak. He has influenced design with Hobie in the mid-1970s, and created Scabs Skate Gear in 1984. Dale rode for Bayside skateboard team in the early 1960s and rode for other teams, including Hobie. He was the creator of the "Sausage Man" deck, a popular board in Europe, and worked with Carol Weber in producing the Weber Longboard in the 1990s He has been designing skaters for decades with Madrid and many others. He pays tribute to the sport by being one of the top collectors and historians of skateboarding, with a collection of over 700 boards. See his website at www.skateboardhistory.com.

Overhead view of the Skate Lab. *Courtesy Todd Huber. Photo: Rhyn Noll*

Courtesy Todd Huber. Photo: Rhyn Noll.

Just some of the 2000 boards at Skate Lab. *Courtesy Todd Huber. Photo: Rhyn Noll*

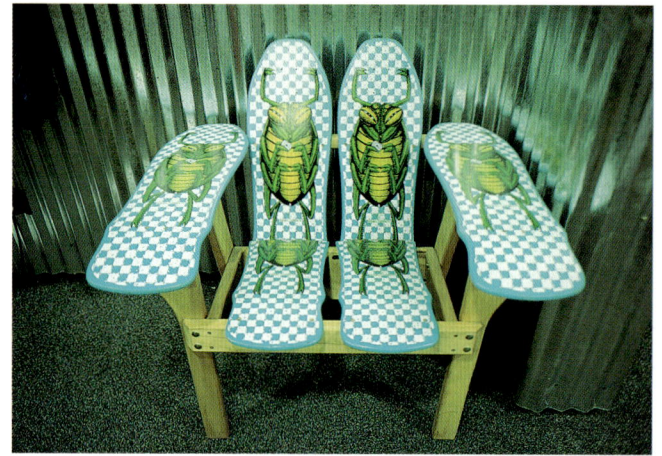

Skateboard Chair, Skate Lab Museum. *Courtesy Todd Huber. Photo: Rhyn Noll.*

Todd Huber currently possesses what has got to be the largest collection of skateboards and memorabilia I have ever seen. He runs Skatelab in Simi Valley, a massive indoor skate park and museum. Todd has over 2000 skateboards and other memorabilia. When you enter Skatelab, skateboards line the roof as well as the walls. Photos, history—you name it, he's got it. The collection is so impressive that it was declared a legitimate museum by the California Historical Society. If you like skate history this place is a must! Todd holds this sport's soul as well as its future; his skate park is a forum for both today's and tomorrow's skaters. Visit Skatelab on the web at www.skatelab.com

C.J. Nelson with some air.
Photo: Patrick Trefz.

TOP LEFT:
Luging Photo. *Courtesy Gravity.*

CENTER & BOTTOM LEFT:
Stephen Locelli and Brandon Wolong snowboarding, one of skateboarding's brothers. The relationship is apparent from vert to carve. *Photo: Patrick Trefz.*

TOP RIGHT:
Juleyn Sekon with some apparent vert. *Photo: Patrick Trefz.*

CENTER RIGHT:
Joey Nichols with some air. *Photo Patrick Trefz.*

BOTTOM RIGHT:
John Meeks with five over. *Photo Patrick Trefz.*

Conclusion

When I think back about my personal skate history, I would be willing to bet none of us considered the gravity of what we were privy to as kids. All things grow and this sport has too. Looking back over one hundred years of history was not always an easy task, but one worthy of the challenge. Just to be involved has been an honor and a privilege. Hopefully this has contributed to the sport's proud heritage. Bringing honor and continuity to what it is we all do, old school or new, was my goal.

What lies in store for the skate industry? Your guess is as good as mine. The sport is one hundred years young and as we sit at the beginning of the year 2000, I can't help but wonder what direction skateboards will roll. One thing is certain, skateboarding is here to stay. Despite several struggles for survival it has not died, but evolved. It will continue to change to accommodate the future. Built on the people who have brought the sport where it is today, the magnificent ingenuity will continue.

The "anything goes" spirit of the end of the 1990s will continue into the new millennium. Small boards, long boards, and everything in-between will find their riders. Skaters will utilize all of their options; old school, new school, longboarders, freestylers, cruising, and skating aggressively are all factions active at the beginning of the new millenniums.

As we begin this century, the sport has finally come of age. Its legacy has come full circle with a portion of today's boarders moving through the concrete discipline to a grass roots frame of mind. Traditional boards and styles honor the sport's beginning and heritage.

I hope that this book has helped to preserve the heritage of skateboarding, to show the connections between all aspects of the sport. Skateboards and skateboarding, past and present, has been defined by each era, beginning with Doc Ball and his pals in 1918 and 1919 and continuing to the present. In writing this book I have gained a new tolerance and respect for every facet of skateboarding and its offshoots. Whether luging, snowboarding, off-road skating, ski-skating, skunnelling, sky surfing, downhill, and sandboarding, they are all partaking in a grand and exciting tradition.

Skate Parks

This is not a complete catalog of North America's skate parks. It is information I have found or been given.

USA

ALABAMA
High Wheels Skatepark, Decatur
Ramp-N-Speed Skatepark, Birmington
Sanctuary Skatepark, Dothan
Sports Extreme, Mobile
UV Sports, Decatur

ALASKA
Gateway Recreation Skatepark, Ketchikan
John Weaver Memorial Skatepark, Fairbanks
Juneau Skatepark, Juneau

ARIZONA
Desert West Skateboard Plaza, Phoenix
Phoenix Skatepark, Phoenix
Randolph Skatepark, Tucson
The Zone Skatepark, Phoenix
Williams Skatepark, Williams

ARKANSAS
43rd Realm Indoor Skatepark, Hot Springs
Kanis Skatepark, Little Rock
Kimmery Skatepark, Hot Springs
North Little Rock Skatepark, North Little Rock
Rollersports Skatepark, Little Rock
Skate Station, Fayetteville

CALIFORNIA
Arcata Skate Park, Arcata
Benicia Skatepark, Benicia
Brickyard Skatepark, Redlands
California Skatelab, Simi Valley

Calpine Skatepark, Calpine
Carlsbad Skatepark, Carlsbad
Claremont Skatepark, Claremont, California
Community Park, Davis
Derby Skatepark, Santa Cruz
Escondido Skatepark, Pleasanton
FGO Skatepark, Pleasanton
Greer Park, Palo Alto
Ground Zero Skatepark, Madera
Hanford Skatepark, Hanford
Huntington Beach Skatepark #1, Huntington Beach
The Lot, Running Springs
Magdalena Ecke Family YMCA, Encinitas
Modesto Skatepark, Modesto
Monterey Bay Sk8 Station, Sand City
Napa Skatepark, Napa
Oceanside Indoor Skatepark, Oceanside
Palmdale Skatepark, Palmdale
San Jose Ramp Club, San Jose
Santa Maria YMCA Skatepark, Santa Maria
Santa Rosa Skatepark, Santa Rosa
Skatelab Skatepark, Simi Valley
Skatepark of La Verne, La Verne
Skatepark of Santa Clarita, Santa Clarita
Skate N Sport, Victorville
SK8 Underground, Moreno Valley
SLO Skatepark, San Luis Obispo
Skate Street, Ventura
South Lake Tahoe Skatepark, South Lake Tahoe
Temecula Skatepark, Temecula
Vans Skatepark, Orange
Visalia Skatepark, Visalia
Yuba City Skatepark, Yuba City
Wheelhouse Skate Center, Hemet

COLORADO
Alamosa Skatepark, Alamosa
Amco Skatepark, Grand Junction
Anderson Skatepark, Wheat Ridge
Apocalypse Skatepark, Boulder
Arvada Skatepark, Arvada
Boulder YMCA Skatepark, Boulder
Breckenridge Skatepark, Breckenridge
Brighton Skatepark, Brighton
Fort Collins Skatepark, Fort Collins
Colorado Springs Skatepark, Colorado Springs
Craig East Skatepark, Craig
Crested Butte Skatepark, Crested Butte
Golden Skatepark, Golden
Grand Junction Skatepark, Grand Junction
Greeley Skatepark, Greeley
Hanger Skatepark, Denver
Idaho Springs Skatepark, Idaho Springs
La Junta Skatepark, La Junta
Salida Skatepark, Salida
Steamboat Skatepark, Steamboat
Telluride Skatepark, Telluride
West Lake Skatepark, Grand Junction
Wheat Ridge Skatepark, Wheat Ridge

CONNECTICUT
Axis Boardsports, Brookfield
B-17 Skatepark, Woodbridge
Compo Beach Skatepark, Westport
Connecticut Bike and Skate, Bristol
Eastern Pulse, Milford
Extreme Skatepark & Inline Skatepark, Wallingford

DELAWARE
Newport Skatepark, Newport

FLORIDA
Astro Skating Center, Tarpon Springs
Badlands Skatepark, Altamont Springs
Boca Raton Skatepark, Boca Raton
Brotherhood Skatepark, Ft. Meyers
Class Room Skatepark, Callaway
Eagle Lake Skatepark, Wilton Manors
Edge Skatepark, Wilton Manors
Escape Zone, Navarre
Kona Skatepark, Jacksonville
Lakeland Skatepark, Lakeland
Madd Chuck's Skatepark, Panama City Beach,
Sanctuary Skatepark, Naples
SFX Skatepark, Pembroke Pines
Skate Asylum, Jacksonville
Skate Park of Tampa, Tampa
Skateshack, Pensacola
Stone Edge Skateboard Park, South Daytona

GEORGIA
Etowah Skate Center, Rome
Heaven Skates, Woodstock
North Georgia Skatepark, Dalton
Peachtree City Skatepark, Peachtree City
Ramp-N-Roll Skatepark, Warner Robins
Skater's Extreme, Snellville
Skate's N Bruises, Cartersville

HAWAII
Aala Park, Honolulu
Ewa Beach Skatepark, Ewa Beach
Hickham Hangar, Pearl Harbor
Kahului Skatepark, Maui
Pililaau Community Park, Waianae
YMCA Kapahulu Skatepark, Honolulu

IDAHO
Cour d'Alene Skaters' Park, Cour d'Alene
D.A.R.E. Skatepark, Caldwell
Ketchum Skatepark, Ketchum

ILLINOIS
Drop In Skatepark, New Lennox
Jewett Public Skatepark, Deerfield
Kankakee Area YMCA, Kankakee
Lattof YMCA Skatepark, Des Plaines
Mokena Skatepark, Mokena
Private Indoor Terrain, Rockford
Skate Cycle Rollerblade Action Park, Estates

INDIANA
D.K.'s Main Street Skatepark, Kokomo
Just Ride Skatepark, Anderson
Skatepark of Logansport, Logansport
Travel Alternative Skatepark, Indianapolis

IOWA
DS Sports USA, Iowa City
Fort Dodge Skatepark, Fort Dodge
Rampage Indoor Skatepark, Davenport
Stubbuz Skatepark, Clinton

KANSAS
BOARDorLINE Skatepark, Wichita
Hays Skatepark, Hays
Salina Skatepark, Salina

LOUISIANA
Board Stiff Skatepark, Houma
Interskate, Shreveport
Monsoon Skatepark, Baton Rouge
Second Nature Skatepark, Kenner

MAINE
East Machias Skatepark, Ellsworth
Zone, Portland
Inner Sanctum Skatepark, Ellsworth

MARYLAND
Lansdowne Skatepark, Baltimore
Ocean Bowl Skatepark, Ocean City
Rock Hall Skatepark, Rock Hall
Smithsburg Skatepark, Smithsburg
Spicy Skatepark, Whitemarsh

MASSACHUSETTS
Alpine Skatepark, North Andover
Bridgewater Skatepark, Bridgewater
Chatham Skatepark, Chatman
Eight Ball Skatepark, Bellingham
Fairhaven Skatepark, Fairhaven
Nantucket Skatepark, Nantucket
Nickerson Skatepark, Attleboro
Projects Skatepark, Weymouth
Scituate Skatepark, Scituate
Z.T. Maximus, Cambridge

MICHIGAN
Airborne Skatepark, Roseville
Carnes Skatepark, Monroe
K-Zoo Skate Zoo, Kalamazoo
Marquette Skatepark, Marquette

Metro Trend Skatepark, Ferndale

MINNESOTA
Discontent Skatepark, Moorhead
Drop Zone Skatepark, Bemidji
Northfield Public Skatepark, Northfield
3rd Lair Skatepark, Minneapolis
Woodwords YMCA Skatepark, Mankato

MISSOURI
BTB Skatepark, Joplin

MONTANA
Libby Skatepark, Libby
Set Free Skatepark, Great Falls
Shady Lane Skatepark, Kalispell
YMCA Skatepark of Missoula, Missoula

NEVADA
Carson City Skatepark, Carson City
Las Vegas Skatepark, Las Vegas
Park 216, Henderson
Planet Plywood, North Las Vegas

NEW HAMPSHIRE
Alexander Car Skateboard Park, Derry
Exeter Skatepark, Exeter
X Dream, Portsmouth

NEW JERSEY
Alternative Sports Skatepark, Toms River
Casino Skatepark, Asbury Park
City Run Skatepark, Brigantine
Extremes Skate and Inline Park, Bridgewater
Hackettstown Sports Park and Skating Arena, Hackettstown
Jacksonville Chapel, Lincoln Park
Kingpin Extreme Skatepark, Pleasantville
Washington Lake Park, Sewell

NEW MEXICO
Los Alamos Skatepark, Los Almos
Santa Fe Skatepark, Santa Fe

NEW YORK
516 Skatepark, Capague, Long Island
AXIS (Albany Xtreme Indoor Sports), Albany
Board Sports Skatepark, Patchogue
Chelsea Piers, New York
Coming Skatepark, Coming
Cortland Skatepark, Cortland
Island Vibes Skatepark, New York

Mountain Run, Lake Placid
Riverside Skatepark, Manhattan
Rome Skatepark, Rome
Saratoga Springs Skateboard Park, Saratoga Springs
Spinners Skatepark, Macedon
World of Wheels Skate-Recreation Park, Ashford
YMCA of Kingston and Ulster County, Kingston

NORTH CAROLINA
GP Skatepark, Fayetteville
Jaycee's Park, Greenville
Middle School Skatepark, Wilmington
Ryan's World Skatepark, Raleigh

OHIO
Aggressive Skate, Cincinnati
Brook Park Ramp, Brook Park
Coe Lake Skatepark, Berea
Chenga-World Skatepark, North Ridgeville
Cleveland Skatepark, Cleveland
Dodge Skatepark, Columbus
Everett Skatepark, Newark
Fat Mike's Skatepark, Lorain
Independence Skatepark, Independence
Lorain Skatepark, Lorain
Lunken Airport Skatepark, Cincinnati
Newark Skatepark, Newark
Ohio Surf and Skate, Dayton
Roller World Skating Ring, Pama
Skatopia, Rutland
Smithgrind, Tallmadge
Tiffin Skatepark, Tiffin
Union County Family YMCA Skatepark, Marysville
Willoughby Skatepark, Willoughby

OKLAHOMA
Boards & Blades, Oklahoma city
Grand Lake Skate Zone, Grove

OREGON
Ashland Skatepark, Ashland
Baker City Skatepark, Baker City
Bend Skatepark, Ponderosa Park
Burnside Skatepark, Portland
Campus Life Underground, Medford
Cannon Beach Skatepark, Cannon Beach
Crazy Eight Skatepark, Eugene
Fairgrounds Skatepark, Eugene
Forest Grove Skatepark, Forest Grove
Gresham Skatepark, Gresham
Hood River Skatepark, Hood River
Jubilee Park, Cave Junction

La Grande Skatepark, La Grande
Lake Oswego Skatepark, Lake Oswego
Lincoln Park, Forest Grove
Lincoln City Skatepark, Lincoln City
Ponderosa Skatepark, Bend
Salem Skatepark, Salem
Seaside Skatepark, Seaside
Downtown Skateboardpark, Talent

PENNSYLVANIA
Boards and Blades Skatepark, Boothwyn
Cheap Skates II, Lexington
Extreme Sports Skatepark, Ivyland
FDR Skatepark, Philadelphia
Keystone Skatepark, Lancaster
PA Cheapskates, North Versailles
Penn Skate, Allentown
Shady Skates, Pittsburgh
Shymerville Skatepark, Emmaus
Starting Gate Skatepark, Marshall's Creek
West End Skateboard Park, Brodheadsville
Wheels in Motion, Redding
Wheels Skatepark, Blakeslee
Woodward Skate Camp, Woodward

RHODE ISLAND
Skater Island, Middletown
Two-Pi Skatepark, West Warwick

SOUTH CAROLINA
Carolina Skatepark, Duncan
Easley Skatepark, Easley
Myrtle Beach City Skatepark, Myrtle Beach
Skatepark of Charleston, Charleston
Slab Skatepark, Columbia

SOUTH DAKOTA
Meldrum Park, Sioux Falls

TENNESSEE
Axis Skatepark, Knoxville
Rampage Skatepark, Oliver
XXX Sportspark, Nashville

TEXAS
Blueliquid Skatepark, Los Fresnos
Eisenbergs Skatepark, St. Plano
Freestyle Skatepark, Kennedale
Intellect Rollers Realm, Austin
South Side Indoor Skatepark, South Houston
Team K Skatepark, South Padre Island

UTAH
Grantsville Skatepark, Grantsville
Joe's Skatepark, Orem
Real Ride Skatepark, Salt Lake City
Sandy Skatepark, Sandy
Tooele City Park, Tooele

VERMONT
Blacksburg Skatepark, Blacksburg
Cutting Edge Skatepark, Bennington
Flat Street Skatepark, Brattleboro
Stowe Skatepark, Stowe
Zero Gravity Skatepark, Rutland

VIRGINIA
Chesapeake Skatepark, Chesapeake
Catoctin Circle Skatepark, Leesburg
Hopewell Skatepark, Hopewell
Laurel Skatepark, Glen Allen
Mount Trashmore Park, Virginia Beach
Scott D. Eagles Memorial, Woodbridge

WASHINGTON
Bellevue Skatepark, Bellevue
Bremerton Skatepark, Bremerton
Eastmont Skatepark, Wenatchee
Kelso Skatepark, Kelso
Kirkland Skatepark, Kirkland
Mercer Island Skatepark, Mercer Island
Mount Vernon Skateboard and Roller Hockey Park, Mount Vernon
Moses Lake Skatepark, Moses Lake
Omak Skatepark, Omak
PT Skatepark, Port Townsend
SCOOPS Skatepark, Port Angeles
Sea-Sk8 Skatepark, Seattle
Silverdale Skatepark, Silverdale
The Skatebarn, Winthrop
Tacoma Skatepark, Tacoma
Vancouver Skatepark, Vancouver
Winatchee Skatepark, Wenatchee

WEST VIRGINIA
Kanawah Skate Club, Charleston

WISCONSIN
Area 51 Skatepark, Sturgeon bay
The Fishing Hole, Madison
Kenosha Public Skatepark, Kenosha
Oshkosh Public Skatepark, Oshkosh
Telfer Skatepark, Beloit
The Pipe, Janesville

Wausau Skatepark, Wausau

WYOMING
Cheyenne Skatepark, Cheyenne
Gillete Skatepark, Gillete
Green River Skatepark, Green River
Jackson Skatepark, Jackson
Rock Springs Skatepark, Rock Springs

CANADA

ALBERTA
Eckville Skatepark, Eckville

BRITISH COLUMBIA
Abbotsford Optimist Club Skatepark, Abbotsford
Campbell River Skatepark, Campbell River
Chilliwack Skatepark, Chilliwack
Courtenay Skatepark, Courtenay
Cuncan Skatepark, Victoria
Fernie Skatepark, Fernie
Garage Skatepark, Nelson
Gordon Head Skatepark, Victoria
Griffin Skatepark, North Vancouver
Kelowna Skatepark, Kelowna
Ladner Leisure Center, Ladner Delta
Langley Skatepark, Langley
Neutral Zone Skatepark, Maple Ridge
North Glenmore Skatepark, North Glenmore
Revelstoke Skatepark, Revelstoke

Richmond Skatepark, Richmond
Seylynn Skatepark, North Vancouver
Sidney Skatepark, Sidney
Summerland Skateboard Park, Summerland
Westbank Skatepark, Westbank
Whistler Skatepark, Whistler Village
White Rock Skatepark, Surrey

ONTARIO
Beasley Bowl, Ontario
The Boarding House Skatepark, Thunder Bay
Collingwood Skatepark, Ontario
Gravenhurst Skatepark, Ontario
Kitchener Skatepark. Kitchener
Nowhere Skatepark, Pickering
Rampage Skatepark, Ontario
Sarnia Skatepark, Sarnia
Sud Skates, Catharines

QUEBEC
Riki Skatepark, Rimouski
Tazmahal Skatepark, Montreal

SASKATCHEWAN
Archibald Arena, Saskatoon
Regina Skatepark, Regina

YUKON
Second Heaven Skatepark, Whitehorse

Glossary of Skateboard Terms

180: One Hundred and eighty degrees. Measure of rotation. Used to describe skate-boarding tricks

360: Three hundred and sixty degrees. Measure of rotation. Used to describe skate-boarding tricks.

5-0: Grinding with the axle of the rear truck on the edge of the object.

50-50: Grinding with the axles of both trucks on the edge of the object.

900: Two and a half revolutions or rotations. Achieved by Tony Hawk in 1999.

A: A measurement for the hardness of skateboard wheels.

ACID DROP: Skating off the end of an object while ollieing or touching the board with your hands.

AIR: When skateboard and skater leave the ground/ramp without ollieing.

ALLEY-OOP: A move in which you turn one way while rotating another.

ARMOR: Your pads.

ANTI-ROCKER: A wheel setup with small wheels in the middle of the skates and larger wheels on the outside. Supposed to allow easier grinds due to the bigger area between wheels.

AXLE: The metal rod running through the hanger, with the wheels screwed on either end.

BACKSIDE: Originated from surfing, the direction you turn if you are traveling up a wave and turn so your back faces the wave. Used to describe your direction of rotation in skating. The opposite of frontside.

BACKSLIDE: A Grind using only the back foot, balancing carefully on the boot and frame.

BACON IN THE PAN: When you wipe out major on a ramp. You slide around and shrivel up like frying bacon.

BANANA: Another term for switch.

BAR: Name for grinding bar or rail.

BANK: An elevated surface. A common urban form of ramp.

BASEPLATE: The flat part of the truck that fixes to the board via four drilled holes for truck bolts. Also has an area to attach a pivot cup and kingpin.

BEARING: The part of the board that bears the friction of movement. There should be two contained within each wheel.

BERANI: A front flip with a 180 in it.

BIGSPIN: A 360-degree shoveit with a 180-degree turn in a backside direction.

BIO: Sideways spin.

BLINDSIDE: A trick where you turn away from the grinding object to grind it.

BLUNT: Going up over an object and landing with the tail along the edge of the object and the rear two wheels on top of the object. The board should then be pointing in a near vertical position.

BOARD: Main platform area of a skateboard.

BOARDWALK: A topside soul with back foot rolling on its toe.

BONED: Pushing the board out in front and pointing downwards in mid-air.

BONELESS: Take the front foot off the board and grab the board with your hand. With you back foot still on the board, jump up. Then place your front foot back on the board and remove your hand before landing.

CAB: Fakie 360

CABALERNO: A backflip with a 180 in it.

CAMEL: Toe-Tap

CASPER: With the board upside down, place the front foot underneath the board and back foot on the tail, pointing the board into the sky.

CAVEMAN RAIL: A rail that is really high and hard to get on.

COMP: Short for competition.

CONCAVE: The contour given to decks. The concave will dip down from the left to right and should be asymmetrical. Provides strength to the board and aids the skater when performing tricks.

COPER: Protective covering for the truck that attaches to the hanger. Protects the truck against grinding.

COPING: Metal piping running along the top edge of park bowls and ramps. Provides a longer life to the ramp and increases the range of skateboarding tricks.

CURB: Concrete upcropping at the edge of roadways. What coping is to ramps, curbs are to streets.

CURB GRIND: A grind that is done on a curb.

CUSHION: Donut-shaped rubber components found on trucks, slotted onto the king-pin. Provide steering and act as shock absorbers. Can be bought in a range of colors and hardness. Two are needed per truck; the one that's slightly cone shaped fits furthest up the kingpin.

DARKSIDE GRIND: A grind that flips the board upside down; the rider stands on the underside of the board.

DECK: Main platform area of a skateboard.

DELAM: Damage done to a deck through skating as a layer is chipped from the ply-wood deck. The thin layer removed is called a "delam."

DISASTER: Placing the rear wheels on top of an object with the rail of the board on the edge. The front two wheels are therefore hanging off the object.

DOUBLE ORE-IDA: Vert trick in which you alley-oop 720.

DOWNHILL: Skating as fast as possible down the steepest of hills for the greatest of adrenaline rushes. Has also developed into a separate area of skateboarding with special boards and techniques.

DROP BEARINGS: Loose ball bearings used in the '70s.

DROP-IN: When you enter a ramp from the top.

ELBOW: One mini-half pipe placed at an angle next to another one, allowing you to transfer between them.

EGG PLANT: Handplant where you plant only the outside hand.

EMB: Embarcadero, San Francisco, America. Once the greatest urban mecca for skateboarding.

EXPRESS AIR: Grabbing the inside of the skate with the same side hand.

FAKIE: Traveling backwards. Driving a car in reverse is, in effect, going fakie.

FARSIDE: A grind where you go over the bar and land on the "farside" to start grinding.

FAST SLIDE: A grind using only the front foot.

FAT: Adjective meaning high or far. Used to express a skateboarding trick that is performed over a long distance or a great height. Also spelled "Phat."

FEEBLEGRIND: Grinding with the rear truck while the front truck goes over the top of the edge of the object, putting the board at a slight angle to the direction of movement.

FLATLANDER: A skater who skates only street and no vert.

FLIP: Developed from freestyle skating. It involves the board turning upside down in a variety of combinations. A flip is generally considered to be a complete flip over to land back on the wheels.

FOCUS: Snapping the deck into two pieces. It was once "fashionable" to do this when you became frustrated, said to be conjured up by a part of the industry who wanted to sell more boards by making people think it was cool to focus the board they were riding.

FREESTYLE: An area of skating that has now become part of street and vert skating. Used to be performed on low-riding, skinny boards. Tricks consisted of numerous balancing tricks, flips, and shove-its.

FRONTSIDE: Originated from surfing, the direction in which you turn if you are traveling up a wave and turn so you face the wave. Used to describe direction of rotation in skating. The opposite of "backside".

FUNBOX: A platform object with banked sides plus a handrail, if you're lucky.

GOOFY: You skate goofy if you skate with your right foot forward. The opposite of regular.

GRAB: Using your hand to "grab" onto your board.

GRAPHICS: The artwork on the bottom of a deck. It helps in telling one deck from another.

GRIND: Moving along the edge or on top of an object with the axles of both trucks.

GRIPTAPE: A sticky-back sandpaper material. Usually black but can be bought in a range of colors, even clear. It is used to cover the top of the deck, to create friction that aids the skater.

HALF CAB: Going from skating backwards to skating forwards.

HALF PIPE: A ramp, usually made out of wood, that looks much like half of a pipe.

HANDPLANT: A form of handstand where the board is held in the air either by a hand or feet.

HANDRAIL: Common urban feature, designed for holding on to while traveling up and down stairs, though used by skaters for a whole range of tricks.

HANGER: Part of the truck that gets the most abuse. When you grind, you are grinding along the top of the hanger. Contained inside the hanger is the axle.

HEELFLIP: Flipping the board with your heel. Your front foot should move up and across the board, flipping it in the opposite direction of a kickflip.

HELMET: Protective equipment for your head. Nearly always used in vert skateboarding.

IMPOSSIBLE: Freestyle trick invented by Rodney Mullen. Consists of spinning the board around either foot.

INVERT: Going upside down on the ramp and doing a handstand.

INDYGRAB: Grabbing the board in front of you with the rear hand.

JAM: Getting a load of skaters together for a skateboard session.

K-GRIND: Stands for "Crooked Grind". Grinding along on the leading truck without having the board over the object.

KICKFLIP: Flipping the board by kicking it.

KICKTURN: Rotating on the rear wheels of the board with the front wheels raised from the surface.

KINGPIN: The bolt that holds the hanger, cushions and baseplate together of the truck.

KINK: Used to describe handrails. A kink is the changing of the handrail's angle. A handrail that runs down a set of steps then goes horizontal is a two-kink rail.

LAUNCH RAMP: A portable street ramp made for skaters to launch from.

LIP: The top edge of a ramp.

LIPSLIDE: Sliding along on the rails of the board with the rear wheels going over the object.

MANUAL: What people commonly call a wheelie—traveling along while balanced on the two rear wheels.

McTWIST: 540-degree backside air with a mute grab. Invented by Mike McGill.

MELLONCOLLIE: While in midair in an ollie, grabbing the board behind you with the leading hand.

MINIRAMP: A ramp (two transitioned banks facing each other with flat bottom and platforms) that does not have any vert, usually around 6 feet in height.

MM: Millimeters. The standard measurement for the diameter of skateboard wheels.

NOCOMLY: Old-school street skating trick. There are many variations but it basically means to travel along with the rear foot on the tail, then place the front foot on the ground and pop the board into the air.

NOLLIE: Follows the same concepts as an ollie. While travelling along, place the front foot on the nose and pop up into the air using the nose (rather than the tail in an ollie). The exact same as a switch-stance fakie ollie.

NOSE: The part of the deck in front of the front truck. Opposite end to the tail.

NOSEGRAB: Grabbing the front of the board (nose) with the leading hand.

NOSESLIDE: Sliding along an object using the underside of the nose.

OLLIE: Invented by Ollie Gelfand and brought to the streets by Rodney Mullen. Taking air without using your hands. The basis for most skateboarding tricks.

PADS: Protective equipment for the knees and elbows. These are mainly used by vert skaters or and in competitions with insurance worries.

PARK BOWL: A simulated pool or bowl-shaped area in a skatepark.

PIVOTCUP: A plastic cup that fits into the baseplate and stops the metal hanger from coming into contact with the metal baseplate.

PLATFORM: An elevated flat surface.

PLY: Short for plywood. The most commonly used material for the deck. Usually seven-layer ply.

POPSHOVEIT: A shoveit mixed with an ollie. Enables shoveits to be performed higher.

PRO: A professional. Someone who gets paid by a company to skateboard. Often has his/her own signature model deck of which he/she has a percentage of all sales.

QUARTERPIPE: One side of a mini ramp or vert ramp, not as wide. Used for gaining speed on a street course or practicing ramp tricks.

RAILS: On the underside of the board. The edges of the deck running along each side of the trucks. They used to be plastic strips attached to the bottom of the board but now are pretty much built in.

RAILSLIDE: Sliding along an object on the part of your board that is the bottom between the trucks.

REGULAR: You skate regular if you skate with your left foot forward. The opposite of goofy.

REVERT: Finishing a trick coming out forwards, then quickly sliding round 180 to come out backwards.

RIPGRIP: Thin sticky back sponge material stuck onto the bottom of boards to give your fingers some grip when grabbing.

RISER: Usually made from plastic or rubber. Fits between the deck and baseplate of the truck. Helps absorb shock.

ROCKANDROLL: Ramp trick. Go up to the lip and push the front truck over it. Stall, then turn 180 back down the ramp.

ROLL-IN: To skate along the platform of a ramp, over the lip and down onto the transitions. The part of a ramp that curves onto the platform is also called a roll-in, because of the purpose it serves.

RUBBER: Another name for bushings.

SADPLANT: A variation of a handplant where your grab the inside rail and straighten your front leg.

SAUSAGE GRIND: Grab your tail while doing a smith grind on your front truck.

SESSION: The act of skateboarding.

SHOVEIT: Turning the board without turning your body, so the board spins round under your feet.

SKETCHY: A term used in dangerous situations, usually meaning unsure.

SLALOM: Zig-zag motion that skiers do, except on hard ground usually with a dedicated skateboard.

SLAM: Another word for falling off your board and hurting yourself.

SLAPPY: Doing grinds along such things as curbs without ollieing onto it.

SLICK: Special plastic layer fixed to the bottom of a deck, supposed to aid sliding.

SMITHGRIND: Grinding with the rear truck while the front truck runs along the side of the object, not over the top. The center of the board my also be touching the edge of the object.

SNAKE: If you're skating an object in which only a limited number of people can skate, a snake is the person that seems to have more goes than anyone by jumping the naturally occurring "queue".

SNAKERUN: Twisting path with banked sides.

SPACER: A small hollow cylindrical object, usually made from metal, placed between two bearings inside a wheel.

SPINE: If two ramps are back-to-back and do not have a platform at the point of connection, the upside down "V" shape is called the spine.

STALEFISHGRAB: Grabbing the board behind you with the rear hand.

STANCE: Either regular of goofy. The way in which you stand on your board.

STOKED: The feeling of doing something well.

STREET-SURFING: A traditional old-school approach to skateboarding that emulates surfing style.

SWITCHSTANCE: The art of skating the stance that you did not learn to skate with. If you do tricks skating goofy, to skate switchstance you must perform tricks with a regular stance, and vice-versa.

TAIL: The part of the deck behind the rear truck.

TAILGRAB: Grabbing the rear of the board with the rear hand.

TAILSAVER: A piece of plastic that attaches to the underside of the tail, designed to prevent wear and tear on the tail.

TAILSLIDE: Sliding with the tail of the board upon the object and the rest of the board hanging off the object, without having gone over it.

TECHNICAL: The name given to complex skating.

THRASHED: The wear and tear of an object due to skateboarding.

TOSS: Such as "product toss" or "sticker toss". An event usually found at sponsored competitions where products are thrown to the crowd.

TRANSITION: Part of a bank/ramp that inclines in an upward direction.

TRUCK: Fixes to the board, and the wheels fit to the truck. A complete truck is made up of a baseplate, hanger, axle, kingpin, cushions, two special washers and two bolts for the axles.

TRUCKBOLTS: Keeps the truck attached to the board.

TWEAK: To point the board in a different direction than normal.

VERT: Part of an inclined surface that is vertical in gradient.

WALLIE: Skating on to, up, and over a street object.

WALLRIDE: The act of skating up a vertical wall.

WAX: Used to make objects increasingly slippery for skateboard tricks.

WHEELSLIDE: The technique of slowing down without putting your feet down. It is what people may commonly call a skid.

WOOD: The material used for decks.

WRISTGUARD: Protective equipment for the wrist. A type of glove containing a plastic/metal splint running along the underside of the wrist onto the palm of the hand.

Bibliography

Skate Boarder Magazine. Surfer Publications Inc., Dana Point. Cal. 92629

Big Brother Magazine. 8484 Wilshire Blvd. Suite 900, Beverly Hills, Ca.

Trasher Magazine. High Speed Production, 1303 Underwood Ave. San Francisco, Ca. 94124

Skateboarder Quarterly. Surfer Publications, Dana Point. Ca.

Longboarder Magazine. Surf Safari Inc. San Clemente, Ca. 92672

Davidson, Ben. *The Skate Boarder Book*. Grosset and Dunlap Inc., 1976.

Skateboard Handbook. Cowboy Star Publications, 1975.

Wild World of Skateboarding. Argus Publishers Corporation, Wilshire Blvd. Calif. 90025, 1977.

United States Patent Office, Washington D.C.

IMB Intellectual Property-Internet Research

Trans World Skateboarding Business. Times Mirror Magazines, 353 Airport Road, Oceanside Ca. 92054

Brooke, Michael. *The Concrete Wave: The History of Skateboarding*. Toronto: Warwick Publishing, 1999.